EXCUSE ME: DO YOU WORK HERE?

A Workplace Devotional for People Who Wish They Had Called Out Today

Vicky L. Rich

Lucky Bird Publishing

Copyright © 2023 Victoria Rich (writing as Vicky L. Rich)

All rights reserved.

No part of this book may be reproduced, or stored in a retrieval system, or transmitted in any form or by any means, electronic, mechanical, photocopying, recording, or otherwise, without express written permission of the publisher and author.

The King James Version (KJV) of the Bible was utilized for this devotional. It is public domain and available for free public use in the USA.

Scripture quotations marked (NLT) are taken from the *Holy Bible*, New Living Translation, copyright ©1996, 2004, 2015 by Tyndale House Foundation. Used by permission of Tyndale House Publishers, Carol Stream, Illinois 60188. All rights reserved.

Names have been changed, and certain small details were changed to preserve privacy and anonymity in examples and stories that were shared within this book.

Table of Contents

i. Introduction *9*
ii. About these Devotions *13*

I. The People in Your Workplace
- Why Are They Like This? *17*
- The Employee You Know the Best *24*
- At Least I'm Not Like Them *30*
- The "We Are Family" Workplace Culture *36*

II. Dysfunctional Workplaces
- Uproot It *42*
- Grow, Anyway (and Keep Building) *51*
- I Didn't Come Here to Make Friends (*or* Leave the Light On) *57*
- FYI *66*
- This Isn't Working *72*
- Not This Again *80*
- Coping with Change Fatigue (*or* Whose Idea was This?) *86*
- Gossip in the Workplace *92*
- Gripe Squad *97*
- Say *Hello* to Them, Anyway *101*
- Micromanagement & You *106*
- <u>This One is for the Supervisors:</u> Micromanagement & You & Them *115*
- Stress & Rest (*or* Overcoming Hurry Sickness) *121*
- Speak to Your Mountains *126*
- You Are Not Your Mistakes (and You Are Not a Mistake) *130*
- A Fresh Victory Over the Past *134*
- Quiet Quitting & Feeling Unappreciated *140*
- What's Good? *145*

III. When You're Not at Work
- Silently Overwhelmed   *151*
- Feeling Left Behind & Off-Track (*or* Who is Your Shepherd?)   *156*
- Your Worth Beyond a Job (Dealing with Unemployment)   *162*
- Don't Forget to BLOW (**B**uild a **L**ife **O**utside of **W**ork)   *170*

IV. Moving Up or Moving On?
- So You Want to be a Boss (But Do You Want to be a Leader?)   *175*
- Imposter Syndrome (*or* When You Doubt You Can Do It)   *181*
- Sing a New Song   *186*
- Who Will You Help? (When Things are Better)   *189*

  o TL;DR   *194*
  o About the Author   *196*
  o Sources Utilized   *197*

Dedication

This book is dedicated to the one Jesus loves (hint: that's the Apostle John).

(Second hint: That's you, too. You're the one Jesus loves.)

Author's Note

Within these pages, I'm going to be honest, open, a little silly, but as transparent as possible.

I know I wrote this devotional, and I have done my best to give honor to God while writing it, so that means that I must state one thing – right at the beginning of our devotional journey – before we truly begin: no book (including this one), song, event, person, meet-up, movie, relationship, television program, livestream, or anything else can ever take the place of actually spending one-on-one time with the Lord Jesus Christ. Those other things can help us in our faith walk, but ultimately, we find our true selves – and all that we could ever hope to be – while choosing to dwell in the presence of God and worship Him. Everything else that we need springs from Him.

Building on that point, nothing can ever replace reading the actual Word of God. Please, pray and read the Bible. Talk (and listen to) your loving Father. Turn to Him first when you need guidance. That's more important than anything I could ever write.

Introduction

Imagine it: you're walking through the aisles of your favorite store just picking up a few important and necessary items before you head home. You've paused near the appliances and gadgets, internally debating whether to get a mega-sized slow cooker that will take up an entire countertop, a toaster that only cooks bacon, or a butter cutter, but then you hear a voice tinged with urgency ask, "*Excuse me* – do you work here?"

You turn and look at your fellow customer. With a shake of your head, you answer, "No, I don't."

"Sorry!" the customer replies before hurrying away down another aisle – continuing her quest to locate someone who is really, truly on the payroll at this store.

Has this scenario ever happened to you? It's happened to me quite a few times. Afterwards, I always pause and evaluate why I was mistaken for an employee. Am I wearing a lanyard around my neck? Am I wearing the same color shirt as the people who work at the store – accidentally complying with their uniform policy? Am I giving off an *I Work Here* vibe? What exactly is an *I Work Here* vibe?

There was one time when I went to a grocery store in exercise gear and was pushing a cart full of items – but I still got hit with the *Do you work here?* question.

But we aren't the only ones who were mistaken for being someone else.

When Mary Magdalene first saw Jesus Christ after the Resurrection, she thought He was the hired help:

> "Jesus saith unto her, Woman, why weepest thou? whom seekest thou? She, supposing Him to be the gardener, saith unto Him, Sir, if thou have borne Him hence, tell me where thou hast laid Him, and I will take Him away." John 20:15 (KJV)

What happened next in the tomb is a wonderful moment: Jesus simply says *Mary* and she instantly realizes who He is – despite the darkness of the early hours of the day and her teary eyes. Just one word from Him – her own name – was enough to get Mary Magdalene to finally turn around, look at Him, and realize that He was right there beside her.

So, dearest reader, why are we meeting each other via a devotional about challenging, dysfunctional, or downright toxic workplaces?

Because when you tell other people that you're struggling mentally and emotionally at work – you are most often given the advice from family and well-meaning friends to just quit ASAP. For many of us, this is not a realistic nor practical option financially (or for other reasons).

This devotional is for those folks who feel stuck. This is for people who need to sit in their cars for at least fifteen minutes – hyping themselves up – before they feel emotionally strong enough to walk into their company's building and begin their shift. This is for the burnt-out people who feel too guilty to use a sick day and who stay up until 2 AM answering work emails. This is for the person who is trying to do the workload of five people by herself and for the person who needs more resources to do his job, but he's expected to get by on just a broken paperclip and lots of duct tape. This is for the folks who *don't love* being micromanaged, and the ones whose car tires leave skid marks on the pavement as they speed from the parking lot at the end of their workday, and the ones who will *only* miss the office plant when they finally do give their two-week notice (even though they have actual human coworkers).

This devotional is for any employee in any work environment who feels hopeless, defeated, drained, anxious, depressed, exhausted, unappreciated, and overworked most of the time.

This is for the people who wonder if there is something better than showing up to a dysfunctional or tiring workplace multiple days a week.

Since we're all adults here, I think it's okay if I mention the 1996 Disney movie *Muppet Treasure Island*. Near the very beginning of the movie, an orphan boy named Jim Hawkins, along with his best friends – Rizzo (*a rodent*) and Gonzo (*a, well, who knows?*), sing a hopeful song called "Something Better" about a life that isn't just full of dirty dishes, cleaning up after pirates, and other drudgery.

The truth is that there is better, and the great part is that we don't have to wait for our current situation to change for life to be better. There are people who unfortunately believe that God designed for our lives to be characterized by hardship and unhappiness. Yes, life can be really, really hard at times. And yes, Jesus tells us that we'll face trouble, rejection, tribulation, and miserable circumstances sometimes, but He also assures us that through Him we will ultimately have victory [John 16:33] as well as peace, love, joy, and all that we need. Throughout the

Bible and through the work of the disciples, we see Jesus' message of hope echoed.

For people who haven't experienced one, it sounds dramatic to call a workplace *toxic* or *dysfunctional*. But I know what it's like, and maybe you do, too. When you're employed in such an environment, it's easy to feel isolated and to believe you need to deal with everything in your own strength. Both the enemy of our faith and pop culture love for us to believe that we must constantly be Miss Strong and Overly Independent, a flawless Boss Babe, Superman, or The White Knight Who Tries To Never Show Weakness. However, God wants to be our strength. He wants us to rely on Him because He can handle all of what we're going through, and He never gets tired nor overwhelmed.

Whenever you feel alone and like you're in the dark, remember that just because you might not be able feel Jesus' presence in your pain – that doesn't mean He isn't right there beside you. He's there and He sees you even when you can't see Him through your tears. Just like with Mary Magdalene at the tomb.

This devotional is also for the people who are having a bad day or a string of bad days at work – even at an otherwise lovely organization. It happens. It's going to be okay.

I hope that you find encouragement, hope, and love within this book. And that you'll forgive me for the silly parts. But most importantly, may your faith in God's plans for your life grow as you turn through these pages.

About these Devotions

There are 30 devotions (*devos*) within this book – and you can read them at a pace that is best for you (especially since they aren't short like traditional devotions).

All the devotions begin with a verse (called a *key verse*) from the King James Version (KJV) of the Bible (four devotions, and the TL;DR utilize verses from the New Living Translation or the NLT), but feel free to cross-reference the verses using the version that you personally use to study – such as the New International Version (NIV), the NLT, or others. The only change I made to the KJV verses was to capitalize the *H* in *Him* and *He* when the Lord was referenced.

I often mention *customers*, *clients, manager, and supervisor* throughout, but you can substitute these words with ones that are applicable to your workplace. The words *manager, boss,* and *supervisor* are often used interchangeably. Whenever I say *The Word*, I'm talking about the Bible.

The bulk of this devotional is divided into four parts. First, we have *The People in Your Workplace* with devotions that discuss various coworkers you encounter as well as a notorious but well-known kind of workplace culture. Afterall, the people in your workplace (and the people you serve via your work) are ultimately the most important component in your organization. In the second section, we jump into different scenarios you might experience when you're at work, especially if it's a *Dysfunctional Workplace*. The third section of this devotional – *When*

You're Not at Work – focuses on how to spend your free time in a healthier, more balanced way. Finally, the fourth section titled *Moving Up or Moving On?* dares you to see your life beyond your present circumstances.

Instead of defining what is or isn't a toxic workplace in detail, I ask for readers to think critically about their own employment environments and decide for themselves whether it is dysfunctional, toxic, or just difficult. Each person's experience is their own. It might help to take a sheet of paper, divide it into two columns, and list everything that is good/supportive/positive/tolerable on one side and everything that you consider bad/discouraging/negative/unbearable about your workplace on the other side of the paper. Want extra credit? For every negative item on the list, describe what your usual reaction to it is AND whether you can change the negative item you've listed. As an example, let's say you have a coworker who interrupts you often when you speak. Your reaction may be to say nothing about it, but you feel angry and upset the rest of the day every time it happens. Can you change or control a person's habit of interrupting? Not directly, but if it bothers you, you can gently point it out to the coworker – he might not even realize that he does it. Or you can do your best to not allow it to affect you so much mentally and emotionally, especially if the coworker *does* realize he's doing it because interrupting others happens to be his jam.

The aim of the above list is to aid in gaining a balanced view of the place where you work.

Most of the devotions end with questions for you to consider. I encourage the approach of keeping a notebook and a writing tool nearby while you read so you can write down your own reflections. A journal is also a perfect place for any thoughts, words that speak to your heart, or even criticisms/counterpoints that arise while you read. I support you as you read through the issues described within this devotional and brainstorm additional solutions that you can put into practice within your workplace and your life.

The People in Your Workplace

Why Are They Like This?

"Come unto me, all ye that labour and are heavy laden, and I will give you rest. Take my yoke upon you, and learn of me; for I am meek and lowly in heart: and ye shall find rest unto your souls. For my yoke is easy, and my burden is light."

Matthew 11:28-30 (KJV)

Anyone else love celebrations?

"Take Your Cat to Work" Day is on June 19th, "Take Your Dog to Work" Day is on June 23rd this year, and "Wear Your Pajamas to Work" Day is April 16th.

Let's imagine that one of your serious, no-chill supervisors has decided to be the *fun one* now. For some of you, you may have snorted or laughed – but stay with me, we'll do this together. Imagine that this supervisor has decided that he wants to boost employee morale by encouraging his team to partake in all three of these celebrations, but instead of waiting for each of these days to roll around, he's combining them into one action-packed week of fun.

One entire week when you can come in your comfy, sleepy clothes, and all employees' pets – if they are dogs or cats *as per the email* – are welcome every single day.

He also talks about this at the next company meeting. The announcement is met with some employees responding with an unsure

"Uh...okay...?" as they exchange *Is he for real? Are we really doing this?* looks with each other. They, honestly, hadn't read the initial email that first presented this idea, so this is all new to them. Other employees are excited about the announcement: what could be more relaxing and cuter than a workplace full of kittens and puppies?

The week of big fun arrives. There are kittens, puppies, and *wait* – one person brought an iguana, someone else brought their two rabbits (and one has wandered off to do a little exploring), Brenda introduced everyone to her quirky chicken bestie, and I'm pretty sure that Keith brought a snake, which is such a Keith thing to do. *And the pajamas*, oh goodness! There are barefoot yet comfy folks everywhere, animals running amok, people with pet allergies glaring at their coworkers, and everyone is so distracted that nobody has remembered to make a fresh pot of coffee. That's right: a person-who-shall-remain-anonymous filled their mug but left just a sliver of the dark bean juice at the bottom of the carafe before hurrying away from the breakroom. In that person's defense, a temperamental llama named Felicia, who seemed to be watching a soap opera on the breakroom television, did spit at him for being too noisy.

All of that is ridiculous, I know.

Something that could have been good turned into chaos. So many things happening around you in this office – and you're still expected to do your job and do it well.

The thing is, people coming together can indeed be a very good thing, but it will never be a perfect thing – not here in this world. There will always be the potential for miscommunication, misunderstandings, negative conflict, personality clashes, the projection of insecurities, hardened hearts, immaturity, arguments, selfishness, rejection, and hurt feelings when we get together. Things can get as messy as an office full of free-roaming animals. However, there's also the potential for healing, support, growth, forgiveness, improved communication skills, empathy, love, community, answered prayers, and joy when we gather.

Think about your workday. As you walk into your workplace at the start of your shift, what are you bringing? What are you carrying – not in your arms, but within you?

Is it a childhood in which you had to be more responsible and more accountable than any of the adults in your life? Or a relationship in which you felt small and unimportant? Now, you may find it hard to ask for help from coworkers or if you're in a formal leadership role, you may lean on micromanaging and passive-aggressive emails to your direct reports with an aim to make life feel less unpredictable and out of control.

Is it a chronic illness or condition that leaves you exhausted even before you begin your shift? You may feel like you must work three times harder than your coworkers – while skipping your breaks – even though your body is telling you to slow down.

Is it an inability to say *no* or a need to always avoid conflict? As a result, you may overload your schedule with too many commitments – rarely sharing ideas or concerns in the workplace and placing a great amount of importance on pleasing other people at all costs. You may also expect people to know what you need without telling them what you need.

Is it that you were taught that you must be the loudest, most aggressive, and most talkative person in the room – or else risk being walked all over by other people? You may feel like you need to maintain a tough exterior and never open yourself up enough to build friendly, collaborative relationships with your coworkers.

Is it pain – physical, emotional, or mental – that persists so much that it's hard for you to be as patient, focused, and upbeat as you'd like to be? Believe me, I know how coping with pain can take up all your energy.

Is it a past that involves abandonment by a parent, childhood abuse, or domestic violence? I've had coworkers who had these heavy and painful experiences, and sometimes, they chose to wear a shield made of overconfidence and/or work addiction – anything that announced to the world, *I am fine, there's nothing wrong.*

I *was* that employee. The one who would stay up all night with my anxious thoughts, worrying about other people's opinions about me. The one who would spend money I didn't have at 2AM – ordering things that I told myself I needed, not yet realizing that my shopping addiction was my way to cope with loss and to feel worthy, less alone, and in control of my life. I was the employee who found her identity in her jobs, and when I lost my employment, I felt like I'd lost myself.

There's a workplace concept centered around employees being able to bring their whole selves to work. Being able to show up as fully yourself in the workplace means sharing your creativity and ideas, the knowledge and wisdom gained from your life experiences and your background, and the uniqueness that makes you who you are.

Yes, we may carry heavy, unpleasant, or downright painful things with us into our workday, but each of us also brings wonderful things along with us, too.

If Jesus were to walk into your workplace and stand in the center of the organization where you work, He'd easily be able to see every employee's whole self.

He sees your whole self right now. Same for your coworkers.

The fourth Tuesday in April is "Take Our Daughters and Sons to Work" Day in the United States and in Canada. Employers who participate in this holiday want you to bring your little ones into the workplace, but of course, the expectation is that it is for one day only and that your child, for the most part, is supposed to sit quietly beside you while not disrupting your work or anyone else's work.

Sometimes, particularly on a day when many of the people you work with seemed to bring the side of themselves that is supposed to just sit quietly to the side – but instead, there's nothing but disruption, you may wonder, *Why are they like this? Why is working with other people so difficult sometimes? Why do folks have to make things harder than they have to be?*

Not only the people you work *with*, but some of the people you serve. Give a shout right now if you've ever worked in customer service.

Of course, I could remind you of what you already know: we live in an imperfect world. You're going to encounter personalities that clash with your own personality, negative conflict, bad gossip, ineffective leadership, terrible communication skills, favoritism, and other markers of a dysfunctional workplace. Why? Because you work with humans and you are a human – and to paraphrase the Apostle Paul [Romans 7:15-20]: *Sometimes, we know better, but we don't do better, and sometimes, we act like a version of ourselves that we really don't want to be.*

But the reason I landed on as to why working with other people can be difficult?

Only God knows.

Only He knows why that particular person (or group of people) in your workplace behaves the way they do. Only He knows and understands why *you* act the way you do. God sees the full picture.

Our workplace may see us as what's on our name badges, as supervisors and staff, as either a new-hire or as someone who is one tardy away from being fired, as top earners or as "not a team player" – but Jesus sees much more than that.

We have a limited view and opinion about our coworkers. To us, Mike is *only* that grumpy guy who never says anything back when you tell him *Good Morning*. Dana is *just* that boss who is never satisfied with anything you do. Sam is *simply* the kind of coworker who shuts down and refuses to communicate when you gently correct a mistake.

I'm not saying that remembering how very human the humans you work with are *justifies* mistreatment, abuse, or misbehaving. But what I am saying is that we must pray and welcome Jesus into all situations, including a dysfunctional workplace. Who can change hearts, lives, and minds like Him? Who shifts circumstances at just the right time like He does? Who is better at that than Him?

Again, let us think of Jesus walking through our places of employment. He looks out at each of our faces, and as He does, He knows everything we've gone through – and everything we're carrying at that exact moment. In Matthew 9:36, the Word says, "When He saw the crowds, He was moved with compassion for them, because they were harassed and helpless, like sheep without a shepherd."

Jesus shows up and brings His whole self to where we are, and we can bring our whole selves to Him. Yes, even at work. Our workplaces are full of people like us who are carrying heavy burdens and who need a better way to live life on a daily, consistent basis.

A better way to react and communicate. A better way to handle conflict. A better way to lead. A better way to build and maintain relationships.

A better way that enables us to show up as kind, patient, and joyful at work and in our lives beyond work. We also learn to forgive ourselves on days when we aren't the kindest and most patient versions of who we are – and we extend the same kind of grace to others, too, because *hey*, we know what that's like.

Jesus looks at each of us, and He isn't overwhelmed with the weight of what we're carrying. He said that He's more than strong enough – and willing – to carry the heavy stuff for you.

He is our rest on the bad days. He is our peace in difficult work environments.

If you were to look at customers and coworkers (and supervisors, too) through His eyes, what would you see? What would you feel toward the people around you?

Let's take it a step further: if we truly started seeing each other through Jesus' eyes, how would this affect how we treat one another?

The Employee You Know the Best

"...The trouble is with me, for I am all too human, a slave to sin. I don't really understand myself, for I want to do what is right, but I don't do it."

Romans 7:14-15 (NLT)

I remember one night when I was out with two of my lady friends (currently, I like the phrase *lady friends* instead of *girlfriends* – it sounds so regal and sophisticated), Diana and Candice. Candice and I listened sympathetically as Diana told us about another romantic prospect that had fizzled out. Being supportive friends, of course we assured her that she was lovely and that it was those guys who had the problem.

But Diana responded with a *NO!* with such emphasis that I was taken by surprise. We looked at her and truly listened as she continued, "*No.* There has to be a reason I keep attracting and being attracted to the same kind of people: ones who aren't good for me. Maybe I need to take another look at myself – at what I'm doing."

I know, I know, this isn't a romantic relationship devotional. However, at the heart of this entire book is a focus on relationships: the relationship you have with God and the relationships you have with the people in your workplace.

But there's another relationship that is also important: the one you have with yourself.

In the organization where you work, you are the employee you know the best.

My friend Diana was right, of course: we begin to understand our own experience by first nurturing our relationship with God, and secondly, by getting to know ourselves.

When we accept a position at a company, it is helpful to examine what expectations we have before our first day on the job. We should also check in with ourselves and assess our needs and beliefs. You can and should reevaluate your expectations, needs, and beliefs throughout your time at the company.

Here are examples of some questions to ask yourself:

- **What do I expect to gain from the actual work I do?** Is it a sense of purpose? To feel useful to the organization's goals? Attainment of new skills that you can use in your next position? Ability to move up in the company? Opportunities to serve your community? A big enough paycheck to take care of yourself (and your family)?

- **What do I expect from my coworkers?** For everyone to interact like mature, well-adjusted grown-ups most of the time? Support, respect, and connection? Friendship? Rarely (if any) disagreements? People who will just leave you alone and let you do your work in peace?

Now, here's where we add in what you know about yourself. Let me ask you a few questions:

- **How do you react to constructive criticism?** How do you handle correction? Does the notice that it's time for your annual job evaluation motivate you to hide under a table in the breakroom?

- **How do you usually handle conflict and disagreements?** Do you shut down, avoid the person, talk it out, or try to "win" against the other person at all costs? Do you hide under a table in the breakroom?

- **Are you accustomed to working in dysfunctional workplaces?** What does a healthy work environment look like to you? Does your boss hide under a table in the breakroom instead of leading and supporting the staff through difficult moments in the workday?

- **What do you believe about your fellow humans in general?** That we are all imperfect but worth getting to know? That you're going to get hurt if you let anyone too close? That there are people in the world who genuinely want to help others? That people will abandon you when you need them the most?

- **How do you cope with difficult, stressful circumstances?** Where, to whom, or to what do you turn to first for comfort?

- **What's your current outlook on your life?** Do you believe you're stuck and stagnant – or are you just going through a rough patch? Do you believe you're behind in life? What does the Word say about what's possible? Are you in agreement with God's Word – or do you let society determine your potential and limitations? If God says you're right on time and ready, but the world says you're too old/too young and don't have the right stuff – who do you tend to believe?

- **When it comes to interpersonal relationships, what are your strengths?** Do you pray about problems and address them with the people involved, when necessary? Can your upbeat personality lighten the mood in the room? Are you a great problem-solver? Are there other strengths you have that aren't listed here?

- **When it comes to interpersonal relationships, what are your opportunities for growth (i.e. weaknesses)?** Do you hold grudges and struggle to forgive people for small offenses? Do you shut down and refuse to talk for hours when someone disagrees with you? Do you expect an uneven amount of attention from other people? Are there other opportunities for growth that you have that aren't listed here? (By the way, there's no shame in the word *weakness*, but I thought I'd use a phrase you'd hear in the workplace.)

My dear new friend, how can we talk about and take a closer look at our coworkers without taking a closer look at ourselves? All the questions listed above are just a starting point – a way to begin the process of deepening our self-awareness.

(Also, I cannot emphasize this enough: when we look closer at ourselves, we aren't aiming to be mean to ourselves. This is also not a suggestion to get stuck in a self-help bog. There's nothing wrong with self-improvement, but we must avoid thinking we need to constantly be "fixing" ourselves.)

If we expect zero conflict and unyielding perfection from the people in our workplaces, we need to adjust our expectations *a lot*. If we believe that a good day is a day in which *everything* goes smoothly and everyone says only the right things, then we'd have more good days if we adjusted our mindset – not allowing one bad moment or one negative interaction to ruin the entire day. If we remember that words have power, we'd be careful about how we talk to ourselves (and to others). If we know what healthy and realistic interpersonal relationships look like and feel like, we will recognize when we're involved in one that will cause us harm. If we are self-aware and know our limits, we'll know how much workplace dysfunction is *too much* dysfunction for us to bear – sooner rather than later.

We also won't place unrealistic expectations on other people nor on ourselves.

Have you ever asked yourself exasperatedly, *Why did I just say that?* or *Why did I act that way?* In our key verse for this devo, the Apostle Paul reflects on himself and on his own behavior. Through his words, we see him acknowledge that he, too, often messed up and made mistakes. Paul was aware, open, and honest with himself about his struggles. However, instead of putting himself down and getting stuck in the muck of focusing only on his flaws, he shifted his focus to God's power and presence in his life.

Knowing yourself – your needs, expectations, beliefs, strengths, and opportunities – will help you to navigate interpersonal relationships better (even in difficult workplace environments). If you struggle with self-awareness or want to gain a deeper understanding of what's going on within you, ask God for understanding. As Psalm 139:23 says, "Search me, O God, and know my heart: try me, and know my thoughts."

Every relationship you have will be even better if God's involved in it. I'm pretty sure that I couldn't love and serve people very well if not for Him – and *I want to love well.*

Lastly, I feel like I need to reiterate this: this devotion is not a suggestion nor an invitation to be unrelentingly critical toward yourself. You have permission to love yourself. You have permission to love others. God's love clings to you.

We don't do condemnation around here.

At Least I'm Not Like Them

"But let every man prove his own work, and then shall he have rejoicing in himself alone, and not in another."

Galatians 6:4 (KJV)

&

"Let us lay aside every weight, and the sin which doth so easily beset us, and let us run with patience the race that is set before us,
Looking unto Jesus the author and finisher of our faith."

Hebrews 12:1-2 (KJV)

Let's chat about that one coworker most of us have or have had: the Curve Setter.

Back in middle school and high school, I remember teachers sometimes grading tests on a curve. What's grading on a curve? If enough students in the class didn't do well on a test, the teacher would add points to each of our grades to give everyone a boost. When we expected that one of our teachers might grade using a curve, we hoped that none of our classmates would do too well because that would take away how many points were added to our own grades on the particular assignment or exam.

I know, I know, that sounds bad. I've been both that kid who "ruined" the curve for everyone else by scoring too high, and the kid groaning because someone else received a perfect score.

Emphasis here on *kid*.

Adult life shouldn't be measured with a curve, but we sometimes slip into doing just that.

What makes a coworker into a Curve Setter? This is the coworker who is struggling with tasks. The coworker who might be taking longer than expected to learn how to do aspects of their job. This is the coworker who might need to be trained and retrained, and if they take a two-week vacation, they may need more retraining because they've seemed to have forgotten how to do *everything* while they were away.

This is the coworker who makes you wonder how they haven't been fired yet.

This is the coworker who tends to say the wrong thing, or the coworker who has less-than-stellar social skills in general, or the coworker who has those personality quirks that several people in the office view as maddening.

And unfortunately, this coworker – the Curve Setter – gives us an ego boost.

As we see Mister or Miss Curve Setter mess up *yet again*, we think, *How could they make such a silly mistake?! I'd never make that mistake.*

Or maybe our very own Curve Setter has opened up to us (or overshared with us), telling us all about the struggles they have regarding their finances, their significant other, and their past unwise choices.

We may politely listen to them and nod at just the right moments to show that we're awake, but inwardly, we might be thinking, *This person is such a mess! At least I'm not THIS bad.*

Now, there are some Curve Setters who aren't giving their best, but there are also Curve Setters in your workplace who are giving their all. There are Curve Setters who are hard on themselves because they truly desire to do well, but for whatever reason, it's taking longer for them to reach their full potential.

Y'all, sometimes the disciples had some Curve-Setter moments.

They were there when Jesus fed over 5,000 people with five loaves of bread and two fish [Matthew 14:15-21]. *He did that.* They saw it.

But when faced with a similar situation later involving a crowd of 4,000 hungry men (plus their families) and having "only" seven loaves and a handful of anchovies, the disciples couldn't see how *the math would math.*

Even though they'd seen this problem already – as well as how Jesus solved it.

In defense of the disciples, how many times have I seen God deliver me out of difficult situations – just to doubt if He'll be able to do it again? God is always able to do it again. Jesus Christ is consistently Jesus our Savior every day, every night, every moment – as pointed out in Hebrews 13:8.

And then there's Peter (formerly called Simon). Can we talk about Peter? *I think we need to talk about Peter.* His timing: sometimes, not the best. His ability to read the room: also, not great. His tendency to take things from zero to one hundred real quick: excellent.

When other people looked at him, they saw impulsive, rash, well-that-escalated-quickly Simon.

Jesus looked at him and saw bold, outspoken Peter (a name He gave to Simon, which means *rock*) – a man who needed grace for his mistakes.

Please don't ever believe that Jesus chose twelve flawless, perfect men to be his first disciples and followers. They were twelve humans with personality quirks and flaws, yet they were exactly who He was looking for. Only with Jesus can someone be flawed and *just right* at the same time.

Honestly, I've been the Curve Setter in a couple of my past workplaces.

When I'm learning new things, my anxiety gets amped up, and as a result, my mind sometimes just goes *blank*. It's a brain fog brought on by stress, leading me to temporarily seem like I don't know what I know.

We aren't aware of what kinds of obstacles or challenges our coworkers are coping with – obstacles and challenges that may affect their performance, their ability to learn, or their ability to recall information quickly.

Maybe he deals with chronic pain or symptoms from a chronic illness.

Maybe she's taking medication or has a medical condition that affects how she processes information.

Maybe they're coping with a rough home environment.

Maybe he's distracted by worries about a sick family member.

Every time I was a Curve Setter, I was already so hard on myself. Eventually, I learned how to give myself grace, but back then, I was continuously berating myself every time I messed up.

Not only that, but I could tell from the looks on my coworkers' faces that they didn't think I was that smart. Praise God that we don't get our identity from how other people see us!

If we need our coworkers (or anyone) to not do so well just so we can magnify our own success, we need to turn our focus back on our own performance and back on how each of us is showing up in our own lives. Our key verses are centered around focusing on Christ, on our own gifts, and on running our own race, rather than spending our time thinking about how slow or fast someone else is running. Notice how the verse tells us to *run, but with patience.* Be patient with yourself and be patient with others.

The Apostle Paul stated, "But they measuring themselves by themselves, and comparing themselves among themselves, are not wise" [2 Corinthians 10:12].

Instead, we can choose a better approach: build the Curve Setter up.

Offer words of encouragement with a smile. Share a story or two with him about a task in your workplace that took you an extended amount of time to learn well. Allow her to show you how to do something (*it doesn't have to be work-related – we are all good at something*). If there's time and your coworker is open to learning, patiently show him how to do a workplace task that he currently struggles with doing. Truly listen to them when they speak. Remember their strengths and what they do get right. Give grace and be patient regarding personality quirks that you may find exasperating.

Have you ever felt like the Curve Setter in your workplace? Think of the coworker you have who is struggling, but who seems to care about doing the best job that they can.

Jesus Christ is our ultimate Comforter and Encourager.

The next time you're working with that coworker whom others compare themselves with by saying, *At least I'm not as much of a mess as him/her* – can you take a moment and encourage that coworker, just like how your Father would?

The "We Are Family" Workplace Culture

"My little children, let us not love in word, neither in tongue; but in deed and in truth."

1 John 3:18 (KJV)

What's the workplace culture at your job? Culture, in this context, refers to the ways that employees communicate, interact, and behave in the work environment on a daily basis. How power and information is distributed is also part of the organizational culture (example: Do multiple employees get together to made decisions or does a manager keep the power to make all important decisions?) It also includes the company's values – both the ones listed on the business' website and the ones that are put into practice in the workplace (*sometimes, the written ones on the website don't match reality*). What are the values in your workplace? Is teamwork valued – *or* one-upmanship where coworkers are focused on outshining each other at all costs? Is there open communication between leadership and the staff, or do you gain information mostly through word of mouth and rumors? Is the culture built on giving grace for mistakes and errors while working together to find solutions, or is shame rampant? How does your company communicate and handle changes?

You may have heard of the "We are Family/We're Just Like One Big Family" workplace culture (also called a "clan" or collaborative culture). Within an organization with this culture, this phrase is used to

36

raise employees' sense of belonging and connection to the organization. High-quality teamwork is the goal. Many people are wary of this culture because they believe that it encourages unhealthy levels of loyalty to the company, unrealistic expectations regarding the amount of support that the company will offer to employees, groupthink, and poor interpersonal boundaries.

If the leadership at the business where you work says, "Oh, we're just like a family here," they are speaking of an ideal employment environment in which everyone supports and accepts one another – replicating the bonds within a supportive family.

Here's the thing about the "We are Family" workplace culture: the company often does not express *what kind of (work) family* you're part of. As we all know, families have different dynamics. Some families are indeed supportive and loving overall, but there are families that are unfortunately, highly dysfunctional. There are families that enjoy getting together for the holidays, and families with members who haven't spoken to each other for a decade. Not forgetting families that are somehow a blend of close, loving, and chaotic – it's kind of a confusing mashup like that homemade trail mix your coworker Holly keeps offering you as she spends your lunch break explaining the nuances between pepitas and basic pumpkin seeds.

The "We are Family" business culture might verbalize the goal of a healthy, kind, interconnected work environment, but we may see certain side effects if the work family has unhealthy dynamics:

- Employees may attach their own identity to the company's identity in a detrimental way. Even when they are no longer satisfied with their job or not making enough to live on – and have no opportunities to move up nor the ability to learn new skills where they are, they may avoid discussing this with their supervisors or be hesitant to seek a job with a different company due to a sense of loyalty.

- Employees may believe that they must always put the company first. They may avoid taking time off – even when they are sick or exhausted. Their own relationships outside of work are neglected (or employees won't put in the effort to form personal relationships that exist outside of work).

- Employees may feel disillusioned when their coworkers are laid off or fired. We often expect unconditional love within supportive families – not to be booted out.

- Employees may avoid sharing ideas – or concerns. No one wants to risk saying anything that may lead to them being excluded or shunned by the workplace family. Even if their ideas might improve some aspect of business operations, or if they have ethical or safety concerns that should not be overlooked. An employee may also avoid standing out or working harder than her counterparts in an underperforming or laid-back environment out of fear of making her less motivated coworkers "look bad."

The bottom line is that no matter how functional and wonderful a family is, no family is perfect. That includes our work families.

This devotion could have been classified in the *Dysfunctional Workplaces* section; however, the "We are Family" organizational culture isn't automatically toxic or bad. Organizations – beginning with its leadership – should create an environment in which staff members feel welcome, respected, and appreciated. Many people do connect with supportive coworkers who become like a "second family." It's amazing to work with people you enjoy spending the day with.

The main issue is when the "We are Family" organizational culture doesn't reflect reality. Do the values that your workplace boasts about to outsiders and to new-hires represent the truth about working there?

Within 1 John and in the gospel of James (and throughout God's Word), there is an emphasis on making sure that our words are supported by actions. God demonstrated His love when He sent His only Son, Jesus, into the world. Jesus demonstrated His love for us through action when He endured the crucifixion. The example given in 1 John 3:11-19 reminds us how love is not just words or promises. Love in motion fills, covers, satisfies, and satiates – it sees a need and does something about it.

Throughout His ministry on earth, Jesus set the example of love modeled through actions again and again.

If you're in a supervisory role, you can set the example of how employees should treat each other by how you treat the people on your team. You can model how to communicate respectfully, how to handle change and conflict in a positive way, how to listen to your team's ideas and concerns, and how to honor rest and breaks. Along with other employees, you can help create (or reinforce) a great organizational culture.

Regardless of what role you have at the company, remember that we are called to not conform to this world [Romans 12:2] – so if your workplace culture includes toxic and unproductive behaviors, you don't need to participate in those behaviors. If negative gossip is popular, you can change the topic or excuse yourself from the conversation. If employees are usually shamed or humiliated over mistakes, you can be gracious and encouraging – focused on problem solving. We take our cues from Jesus – not from how the world behaves.

Even before you're hired, try to find out more about the prospective company's culture. Interviews usually include time for you to ask any questions you may have, so you can ask the interviewer to describe the organization's culture. If they offer a phrase such as "We're all family here" – ask them to give examples of how that shows up via actions in the workplace.

However, if you ask the interviewer about the company culture – and she A) averts her eyes and goes silent, or B) bursts into tears – *then* you may want to rethink whether this company is right for you or not.

Dysfunctional Workplaces

Uproot It

"Rooted and built up in Him, and stablished in the faith, as ye have been taught, abounding therein with thanksgiving."

Colossians 2:7 (KJV)

&

"They are like trees planted along a riverbank, with roots that reach deep into the water. Such trees are not bothered by the heat or worried by long months of drought. Their leaves stay green, and they never stop producing fruit."

Jeremiah 17:8 (NLT)

In our very first devotion, we talked about seeing the humanity in the people around us (and how Jesus always sees the fullness of who we are and who we are becoming). Each of us is going to make mistakes, say the wrong things, and give less than our best sometimes.

When you work with other humans – whether it's serving them or beside them as coworkers (or both), you will sometimes experience interactions that cause you to daydream about moving to a cabin in the middle of nowhere and never interacting with another person ever again.

Is that dramatic? Probably. But surely, you've had one of those days when you're in a great mood, a genuine smile is stuck on your face, and everything seems to be going right, then that one person comes along and says something *(or does something)* that is off-putting or rude – and it feels like the entire day is ruined.

Maybe it was an angry customer being brash and impatient with you.

Or a coworker who made personal comments that caused you to feel uncomfortable.

Or a family member's critical, careless words.

Or a friend's offhanded, offensive remark.

Or a supervisor who often tells you what you're doing wrong, but who never points out what you do right.

How do you react to these situations? How do we keep these interactions – and their potential to affect our emotions and perspective – from ruining our entire day?

First off, it's important to remember that the enemy of your faith wants you to lose your peace. As the Word says, "Be sober, be vigilant; because your adversary the devil, as a roaring lion, walketh about, seeking whom he may devour" [1 Peter 5:8]. He wants you to become – and *remain* – mentally, emotionally, and spiritually disoriented. He wants you to be so distracted by your worries and by what's going on inside your mind so that your entire day off is spent overthinking. He wants you to become – and *stay* – stagnant, pessimistic, and jaded about whether there is any human kindness left in the world. The enemy of your faith wants you to doubt your worth and your identity – and he wants you to hold grudges, withdraw into yourself, and live disconnected from all relationships, even the healthy, positive ones.

In the same way that God will many times send what you need using the people around you (He often works through people), the enemy will also send people to give you what you *don't* need. God sends folks who speak encouraging, hopeful words over our lives. But the enemy sends folks who seem to know exactly what to say to make us feel lonely, dejected, and stuck. There are people who reflect Christ's love back to us, but there are others whose hurtful words or actions dig so deep that we wonder if we're loved at all.

Remember the interaction Jesus had with Peter when Peter told Him that the crucifixion – and therefore, the Resurrection – wouldn't happen? [Matthew 16:22]. Jesus didn't respond by saying *Peter, hush!* – no, He said to him, "Get thee behind me, Satan: thou art an offence unto me. . ." [Matthew 16:23]. He knew that discouragement comes from the enemy.

Therefore, we hold onto the instruction to guard our hearts – or as the King James version states in Proverbs 4:23, "Keep thy heart with all diligence." The use of the word *diligence* reminds us that tending to our heart, to our thoughts (by determining which thoughts to ignore and which thoughts to listen to), and to our emotions is a deliberate action. Guarding your heart from those hope-stealing, day-wrecking comments and insults – and those self-defeating thoughts that spring up – is *work*, but it's good work.

Of course, I needed to mention our own thoughts and how they contribute to our outlook. Because it's not the rude words spoken to us that sink us – it's the thoughts we have *after the interaction* that can drain the peace, joy, and calm from us.

Do you ever find yourself repeating and reliving an upsetting, frustrating interaction in your mind? I know I do.

What can we do instead of ruminating on unkind words or actions that people aim our way?

Uproot them.

Whenever someone insults you, their words can potentially become metaphorical seeds that get planted in your mind, in your heart, and in your spirit. When we focus on and replay those words, we are pushing them down deeper into our soil – and when we believe those words instead of God's truth about us, we're giving those mean seeds sunlight and water. If we're not mindful about what we allow to grow and to take up space within us, weeds will spring up from those seeds – and one day, you'll realize that a majority of what you think about yourself, about others, and about God comes from other people's opinions – not from God.

Sure, what that person said was terrible and *why would anyone ever say that?!* – but their words will not be allowed to thrive and bloom in you. *Nope, not today.* Any words that are not in agreement with what God says about you or words that make you question your worthiness – these untruths need to be uprooted. As it is said in Matthew 15:13, "But He answered and said, Every plant, which my heavenly Father hath not planted, shall be rooted up." Interestingly, this was during a conversation in which Jesus explained how the words we speak can be so powerful because they show the condition of our hearts [Matthew 15:15].

As the second key verse suggests, we will choose to stay green and keep producing fruit even when the heat – in this case, the *heat* is discouraging words – comes our way.

But how do we actually uproot these words?

1. **Challenge the comment in your mind.** Was the statement true – and did it need to be said to you and did it need to be

said to you by this person? Did the comment seem to perfectly target and attack your hidden insecurities, maybe even insecurities that no one (or not too many people) know about? Don't forget that the enemy knows your vulnerabilities. Are the words in agreement with what your loving heavenly Father says about you?

2. **Challenge your own thoughts.** Don't just accept negative thoughts as the truth – just like we can't accept every random comment or judgment as the truth. It's like free food: just because those mystery meatballs are free and being offered to you – that doesn't mean you must get a paper plate stacked with them. And yes, I had to learn this from experience. Just forgo the funky mysterious meatballs – and don't accept everything people say as the absolute truth, especially if it is in opposition to who God says you are or if it makes you doubt His love for you.

3. **Question the purpose and intention of the comment.** What do you think the purpose or intention was behind this person saying those words to you? Does the client have a legitimate reason to be upset? Is it possible the customer is just frustrated with the company – but choosing to take it out on you, the employee? I definitely don't support that behavior, and I cannot justify verbal abuse as an acceptable coping mechanism. However, it does help sometimes to remember that just because it feels personal doesn't mean it is personal. There are times when somebody is having a bad day or they're

in pain – and it is bubbles over onto the people around them. Sure, it would be great if it didn't bubble over onto *you*, but it happens.

In other instances, people will project their own insecurities onto you – sometimes, they don't even realize they're doing it. Often, I need to pray to God and ask Him to help me to see things as they truly are because there will be times when I misinterpret someone's tone, nonverbal communication (such as a frown or body language) or their words. When that happens or when I suspect that's happening, I will also gently ask the other person for clarification (example: *"I'm not sure I understood what was said earlier. When you said X, what did you mean?"* – asked with an even, neutral tone*)*.

4. **Answer the question,** ***Do I know them like that?*** If the hurtful criticism came from a stranger – well, how much do you value the opinion of someone who doesn't even know you? If you highly value a stranger's opinion – why? Here is an equally important question: would someone who loves you and cares about you have said what that person said to you? If the hurtful words came from someone you know on a deeper level – such as a friend or family member, and the person cares about you – you should be able to have a chat with them and explain why their words hurt. They may have spoken without thinking and without intending to cause you pain. If the interaction happened with a coworker or an acquaintance, do you feel comfortable with having that chat with them? Afterwards, are you willing to forgive them?

Forgiveness comes easier when you remember times when you said something you regretted saying. Did someone else give you grace and forgive you after that happened?

5. **Process what was said – then release it.** Okay, you can think about the insult long enough to recover from the shock of *Did they just say that?* But not too long. It's okay to acknowledge that we feel hurt, upset, angry, and other emotions. That's valid. Then we must set those words free so they won't become planted and rooted within us.

6. **Seriously, release it.** Listen, I know this part is hard, which is why it gets two spots on this list. Something that helps me is that I will close my eyes and visualize myself pouring heavy rocks into a box that's beside a river. The rocks represent critical thoughts, mean words spoken by others, and anything else that is weighing me down. Then I visualize myself slamming the heavy lid shut, locking the box, and then *pushing, pushing, pushing* it until I give it one last big shove – and I send the heavy box into the water. As I watch it sink, it symbolizes me letting go of whatever I mentally placed within the box. You can also imagine yourself stomping around in a garden in a funny-looking, straw gardening hat and muddy boots – yanking the weeds that grew from those mean seeds out of the soil.

7. **Step away for a little while.** Within other devotions in this book, I mention how Jesus often needed to step away from the crowds so He could be alone and be renewed by God. After

you encounter a negative and discouraging interaction, try to take a few moments away (if possible) to regain your equilibrium right after it happens. I highly recommend taking time outside in the fresh air and sunshine (*or in the rain – if that's more your thing – no judgment*).

8. **Start again – right now. Today.** An upsetting interaction in your day doesn't mean today was a bad day. We don't need to throw the entire day away due to a few moments of someone else's rudeness. A good day can have negative elements in it – and still be a good day. Maybe 10 AM was rough, but how's 11 AM going? How's your day going at 1 PM? Every hour – every next moment – presents an opportunity for a new start.

9. **Be a kind and self-aware customer/client/visitor.** If you know how it feels to be treated unkindly by the people you serve, let that remind you to be mindful of how you treat employees at other businesses – such as cashiers, restaurant workers, cleaning staff, grocery store employees, delivery drivers, customer service representatives, volunteers, and so on. Also consider the possibility that the employees you're interacting with might themselves work in a dysfunctional environment. We can avoid contributing to that by not unloading any misplaced anger and frustration on them. Let's be one of the bright spots in those employees' day – let's shine God's light in our interactions.

10. **God saw what happened there.** Never forget that your Father sees every interaction you have. You think He didn't see that person mistreating you? You think He didn't hear that terrible comment? Trust Him to help you and trust Him to deal with the other person's heart.

Whenever someone says rude or highly critical words to us, overlooks us, treats us in a careless way, or excludes us, we may expect some kind of closure in the form of an apology – but honestly, you must get to a point when the only two participants you need to get closure and move forward are you and God. If our peace and healing is dependent on other people making things right, apologizing, or even acknowledging how they hurt us – we're going to probably stay pressed, upset, and stuck for a long time, my friend. An explanation or an apology for their behavior would be awesome, but we won't always receive that.

If those words spoken to you don't help you to grow or to deepen your relationship with our loving, grace-filled God, uproot them. Let's stay rooted in Christ – and keep only Christ and His truth rooted in us.

Grow, Anyway (and Keep Building)

"Then answered I them, and said unto them, The God of heaven, He will prosper us; therefore we His servants will arise and build. . ."

Nehemiah 2:20 (KJV)

Do you see the purpose in your position? Or the potential in your placement at that company? It's okay if you don't see the purpose or the potential; in fact, when we work in a difficult, stressful environment, we often focus all our energy on just trying to make it through the workday.

Maybe you deal with rude, angry, uncompromising, demanding, apathetic, and/or unhelpful behaviors from the people around you during an average shift. Or maybe it's a boss who is unrelentingly critical and who doesn't listen to you. Or you cope with never having enough resources and staff. Or your organization is rife with ineffective leadership, arguments and negative gossip among coworkers, constant (and seemingly or *actually* unreasonable) changes mandated by corporate, and/or a workload that leaves you exhausted after you clock out. Or maybe there are even worse problems that you deal with in your workplace.

Not forgetting to mention that each of us has concerns, responsibilities, and worries within our personal lives.

I know that I've prayed to God to remove particular struggles and problems so that I could complete the work set in front of me. If He was willing to answer that prayer – I told myself – *then* I would achieve the goal on time, I would fulfill the dream He placed within me, I would be free to focus on other people who need help, and I would joyfully satisfy the purpose He has for every stage of my life.

If only He would give me good soil with no weeds, *then* I'd grow and bloom.

Yes, doing our jobs and achieving goals would be easier under better circumstances than the ones listed above. However, God usually gives us 1) A purpose for us to fulfill in the season we are in, 2) What we need *when He decides that we need it* to fulfill the purpose (it is based on His timing), and 3) A promise that He will ultimately work all things together for our good [Romans 8:28]. We often encounter the purpose, His timing, and the promise within imperfect circumstances.

When I say imperfect circumstances, please know that *imperfect* can mean different things to each of us. Sometimes, imperfect means that we won't fulfill the purpose based on *when* we thought we would. I've met numerous adults who believe that they are meant to return to school and finish their degrees (or begin college for the first time) – but they were depressed because they wouldn't graduate until they were 30 years old, or 50 years old, or 70 years old. I reminded them that they would be 30, 50, or 70 years old, anyway – whether they returned to school or not – so why not reach for that educational goal?

Imperfect circumstances may mean that you're tired. All the time. When I'm tired, the kind of tired that makes me want to cry like a worn-out toddler – my exhausted body will automatically choose my pillows over purpose every time.

Imperfect circumstances can also mean opposition from the people around you. I'm not just talking about the people who tend to be unkind and grumpy at your workplace. There will be times when the people who are usually on your side – coworkers who are normally supportive as well as friends and family members – will also speak discouraging words over you when you start walking in your God-given purpose and when you start growing.

Grow, anyway.

There was a time when I received an award at work, and a woman who was both a friend and coworker asked me, "What did *you* do to deserve it?"

I wasn't even mad (well, not *that* mad). I knew that I was a hard-working, dedicated employee, and that my friend struggled with the fear of herself not being seen and being left out in life. In the past, I would have agreed with her, shrunk myself to make us both feel comfortable, and said, "I don't know. Our supervisors should have chosen someone else. Why me?" but as I became more secure in the knowledge of who I am in Christ (and more self-aware of my strengths, which God cultivated within me), I answered, "*Why not me?*"

Seeds that were once dormant and comfortable to remain as seeds – when they start growing, it can be intimidating and anxiety-inducing to the other seeds that are still nestled in the soil.

Grow, anyway – but also pray and hope that those other seeds will grow, too.

The book of Nehemiah is a guide for how to handle purpose and goals when faced with imperfect circumstances. The Israelites were returning to their homeland and resettling in Jerusalem, but the wall and gates that protected the city lay in ruins. Nehemiah recognized the importance of the wall, and he, too, returned to Jerusalem – with the goal to unite the Israelites in rebuilding it.

It was a massive construction project involving a lot of work.

It was a *huge* goal.

When God placed this purpose within Nehemiah's heart, did Nehemiah immediately proceed to tell everyone around him about it? No, he didn't. He knew what you may have already learned: when you have a goal, a dream, and/or a purpose, you need to be careful about who you tell about it, especially at first. Nehemiah stated, "And I arose in the night, I and some few men with me; neither told I any man what my God had put in my heart to do at Jerusalem" [Nehemiah 2:12]. Instead of spending his time answering questions and listening to discouraging words before he'd even begun the work, he focused on making plans of how to achieve the goal. He was able to keep his focus in the right place because he didn't tell just anyone about the goal in the beginning. Nehemiah was especially guarded about his purpose in its early stages.

Finally, Nehemiah told the Israelites about the need to rebuild the wall and the gates around Jerusalem. They agreed with him – so they started building together.

Enter the haters/critics: Sanballat, Tobiah, and Geshem. These three men stood by and watched as the goal gradually became a reality – but they laughed at Nehemiah and the Israelites. They mocked the partially rebuilt wall, joking about how even a small animal could break through it [Nehemiah 4:3]. The critics gossiped about the Israelites to others – declaring that the goal was too big, would take forever to finish, and that the builders didn't have the right resources to accomplish what they were trying to do. Sanballat mused, "Will they revive the stones out of the heaps of the rubbish which are burned?" [Nehemiah 4:2].

In other words, he was taunting them by asking, *Do you really think you can build something good from brokenness? Can God actually use what you have and who you are to accomplish His purpose in your life? Can your lives, your joy, your minds, your hearts, and your future be redeemed despite the circumstances you've come from or the ones you are still in?*

Nehemiah's reply to the criticism is shown in the key verse. He ended by telling the haters that what he and the Israelites were doing was none of their business.

They kept building, and the wall was nearing completion. Then the criticism shifted to threats. When the naysayers couldn't thwart the goal with discouragement, they tried fear instead.

So each of the builders kept one hand available to defend themselves from possible attacks and with their other hand, they continued to work on the wall.

Discouragement didn't stop purpose. Neither did fear.

The third way that the critics tried to block the goal?

Distraction.

Sanballat and Geshem asked Nehemiah four times to step away from the wall – and come have a chat with them in a village about 30 miles away from Jerusalem, but he knew that their intentions weren't good.

Every single time, he turned down their invitation by stating, "I am doing a great work, so that I cannot come down: why should the work cease, whilst I leave it, and come down to you?" [Nehemiah 6:3].

Mic drop.

He was reminding them that he had a mission and a purpose to fulfill – and no time for their nonsense.

Through all of this, Nehemiah prayed and depended on God. Ultimately, the wall was completed – despite the people who said it was impossible.

If you are facing overwhelming and discouraging circumstances in your workplace, please remember that God is with you. While you're an employee there, pray that He will show you how to find purpose exactly *where you are while you are there*.

Maybe your purpose at that organization involves helping someone else, or maybe this is the place where you are meant to learn something or connect with someone who will be part of the next stage in your life. Maybe your workday is often terrible, dull, or disheartening, but maybe it provides opportunities, time, or resources for you to pursue dreams that are close to your heart during your free time. Maybe the purpose is as simple as learning how to wait on and trust in God.

So, I know it would be easier to fulfill your purpose if circumstances were better. But there are times when we must build with one hand and grow among heaps of rubbish.

Also, may I add something else that I believe needs to be said: please stop letting yourself give up on your purpose or your goals just because you tried – but you didn't immediately get the results you expected. God helps us to attain the goal, but sometimes, we might not see the fullness of it until weeks, months, or years later. Let's try to avoid planting a seed at night, and then getting discouraged when we don't see an entire tree with fruit by brunch the next day. Trust God. Be patient.

Grow. And keep building.

(To be clear, your discouraging circumstances = the rubbish. I wasn't calling your coworkers rubbish. This is a devotional, afterall.)

I Didn't Come Here to Make Friends

(*or* Leave the Light On)

"Let your light so shine before men, that they may see your good works, and glorify your Father which is in heaven."

Matthew 5:16 (KJV)

&

"Be not overcome of evil, but overcome evil with good."

Romans 12:21 (KJV)

Okay, imagine that it's the end of your workday. A long, tiring, stressful workday. You're burnt-out and have very little energy left for other people. As you skip out the doors of your building into the beautiful sunlight and then dash to your car, you see your coworker, Nicole, standing alone beside her own vehicle with the hood up. It's obvious that she's having car trouble. That's the first problem.

The second problem is, well, you and Nicole don't get along. At all. To you, she's just the *worst*. You're not even sure why she's so unkind to you, but it seems like you won the crown in an unofficial "Nicole's Least Favorite Coworker Ever" pageant on your first day at this company months ago. She makes sure that you know exactly what she thinks of you via her words and actions. Maybe you don't care. Maybe you care a lot. Regardless, you decided to just keep your distance from her in the workplace – only talking to her when it is necessary.

As you skip past her in the nearly empty parking lot, you overhear her ask another coworker if she has jumper cables – and when the coworker shakes her head, a disappointed look fills Nicole's face.

There are jumper cables in *your* trunk.

But you're *so tired*. And this seems like a *Nicole* problem, not a *you* problem. And it's Nicole. And you're not AAA – she should get a membership or something. And there's that Talenti gelato (*or Dolcezza gelato for the five-star-bougie gelato afficionados*) (*or fudge pops for the no-frills ice cream lovers*) in your freezer that's been waiting patiently for you at home all day – it would be rude for you to be late. One does not keep Caramel Cookie Crunch gelato waiting for too long. *And, again, it's Nicole.*

What do you want to do?

But also – what do you believe God would want you to do?

Are your answers to these questions the same?

Our Father loves to give us a gentle nudge (or several nudges) during situations like this. I bet you've felt that Godly nudge before – it's when you sense that God wants you to use an interaction or a situation as an opportunity to shine His light.

Consider when Saul of Tarsus (before he was known as Paul) had his life-changing encounter with God. He was on his way to do one of his favorite things: pursue, persecute, and punish anyone who was a follower of Christ. But Jesus changed his plans – starting with Saul and the men traveling with him hearing the Lord's voice *[For the full account, look to Acts 9].*

After this interaction with Jesus, Saul was changed in two ways: 1) He was now willing to follow Christ, and 2) He temporarily lost his sight.

The Lord – through a vision – instructed a follower named Ananias to go find Saul and lay his hands on him so that he could regain his ability to see. But Ananias' first reaction was to remind Christ about how many awful things Saul had done. Ananias was basically protesting, throwing his hands in the air in confusion, and saying, *Don't You remember how this Saul is the absolute worst? But You want me to go and HELP him?*

Ultimately, Ananias obeys this important nudge from the Lord by seeking out Saul. Then Saul regained his sight and began his work in support of God's people – the same people he formerly abused, harassed, and imprisoned.

Oftentimes, I feel that nudge when I'm walking past someone whom I don't get along well with. My natural urge is to just stare straight ahead and say nothing to that someone. Oh, but then that nudge happens – God gently telling me that I need to say *Hello,* look at the person, and call the person by their name. The nudge reminds me that even when I can't seem to summon up great kindness in that moment, I can at least begin with a little kindness.

Relationships and connection are a big deal in the Word. When Jesus was asked which are the two greatest commandments, He answered by saying that the number one greatest commandment involves our relationship with God and the second greatest commandment concerns our relationships with the people around us [Matthew 22:34-40].

Jesus often talked about friendship. In John 15:9-17, He tells the disciples that they are no longer servants, but are His friends. He further describes the friendship that He has with the disciples and with us, His followers. It includes 1) a love so great that you can dwell within it (I think of His love being like a shelter), 2) a joy that dwells within you (the kind of joy that makes you whole and complete), and 3) the ability to draw close to our Father. Our God does not want us to stay at a distance from Himself – and He doesn't push us away nor call us clingy or too needy when we approach Him. It's quite the opposite. He chooses us, listens to us, connects with us, and loves us.

To Jesus, we're keepers.

When Jesus called the disciples *His friends*, He emphasized what being His friend meant. For His part of the friendship, He was willing to lay down His life for them (and for us). What's our part in this friendship then? How can we possibly match that kind of energy?

Jesus doesn't expect us to match His energy – there's no way we could ever repay Him in equal measure for what He did for us on the cross. Instead, all we need to do to be His friend is to keep His commandments, especially the one about loving other people. He repeats this twice when He talked about friendship – it's that important [John 15:12,17].

Maybe you're not looking to make friends at work. When we're at work, not only do we have things to get done, but we're expected to maintain a certain level of professionalism – and professionalism (for better or worse) often dictates our social interactions. Also, for many people, the word *friendship* denotes a special connection built on mutual and consistent encouragement, trust, openness, psychological safety, and support. You may not feel comfortable becoming friends with your coworkers, especially within a work environment with ineffective, difficult interpersonal dynamics.

Yes, you're a professional – but first and foremost, you are a follower of Christ. He doesn't stand in the front doorway of your home, waving goodbye at you as you drive away to work. Christ doesn't stay behind and sit beside the window, waiting for you to return. Nope. He is with you *everywhere* you go. In the phrase *work/life balance*, Jesus is both in the work and in the life. He's also concerned with the balance. He wants to be part of every area of your life – including the time you spend in your workplace. In fact, even before you get to work, He's already there.

We also need balance in our relationships with the people we work with. If you're a supervisor, being too buddy-buddy with some members of your staff can lead to favoritism and the deterioration of necessary interpersonal boundaries. Also, too much *stickiness* – when coworkers become so comfortable and emotionally connected with each other so that their personal connection overshadows their professional connection when they are at work – can introduce inappropriate conversations, distractions, lost productivity, and relational messiness into the workplace. As examples of things getting sticky, consider a work romance that goes sour *and* petty or that coworker who *intimacy-bombs* you, trusting you with the details of all her deepest secrets even though you've known her for two days – and you only asked could you borrow her stapler. Gradually, you become her daily designated listener: the person she can vent to about deeply personal matters during work hours.

Also, we can't force other people to socialize with us on a personal level or expect everyone to want to be our bestie. Not everyone will like us – and that's okay. Jesus never promised that everybody we meet would love us; in fact, He told us to not be surprised nor shocked by rejection [John 15:18-19].

No matter your job role, a lack of connection between employees can create an apathetic and stagnant environment. A level of connection can be an asset in your organization.

How do we introduce balance?

Perhaps you didn't join that workplace with a desire to make friends – *but* can you at least be a good neighbor to your coworkers? The words *friend* and *neighbor* are often used interchangeably in Scripture. But it helps to look at workplace friendship through the perspective of being neighborly. We can be good neighbors even to people we don't like, can't stand, and who get on our nerves. We can be good neighbors even to coworkers who are dismissive, arrogant, passive aggressive, and unpleasant toward us. We can be good neighbors even to acquaintances. We can be good neighbors even when we weren't at our best yesterday, but thank God there's today and we can do better this time. We show the people around us true love – a love motivated by wanting to be like our heavenly Father – through our good works and by stepping into the gap when we see a need.

Why do we do it? Because Jesus commanded us to do so. The world needs more kindness.

This is not about people-pleasing, nor is this about earning God's love – we can't earn His love, it is given to us freely. This isn't about guilting yourself into going on a picnic with fellow employees who make you feel unsafe in any way. This is also not about forcing yourself to feel warm, fuzzy feelings for every person you meet or about rushing out to buy a bulk pack of BFF necklaces for your coworkers. Remember that love is not just a wonderful feeling within us – love shines best through our actions. Don't guilt or shame yourself if you don't feel how you think you *should* feel. Whenever I sense God nudging me to stretch myself a little and do something good for someone who hasn't treated me well – usually, my first inclination is to groan, complain, and remind Him about the other person's terribleness *(y'all, I said I was going to be honest in this devotional, so there it is!)*.

But then I go and do the thing because deep down, I know it is the right thing to do.

Afterward, I joyfully thank God that I was able to be the person who was given an opportunity to shine His light. And it *does* feel good to help others and to show them that there are people who care. It also feels good to not have my actions controlled by how someone else treats me. I know who my Father is, I know who I am, and I know how I want to show up in this world.

Recall the parable of the good Samaritan [Luke 10:25-37]. A traveler was robbed, beaten, and left beside the road. Two people saw him in distress but passed by without helping him. A third person – a Samaritan traveler – had a different reaction: "when he saw him, he had compassion on him" [Luke 10:33]. He stopped and cared for the downtrodden man.

After telling this parable, Jesus highlighted how the good Samaritan – through his actions – showed how to be a neighbor. Notice how the story is not called *the parable of the good Samaritan and the good traveler.* The parable isn't built upon the goodness of the man who needed help – we don't know whether he was a decent man or not. What's important are the actions of the person who had the ability to either help him or walk away while pretending he didn't see him.

When you see a coworker struggling and you're able to help them, will you stretch yourself at least a little and help? You don't have to begin with great big acts of kindness – even the little bits of kindness make a difference.

Hold up, though.

You may have thought this devotion was over – and we *could* stop there, but we won't.

Many of us have asked God to change the hearts of the people around us – and yes, only God can create lasting change within them. I cannot emphasize this enough, though: if someone is behaving in a way that is dangerous or incredibly harmful toward you, that is not a sign that you need to love harder nor try harder – pray about it, give that over to God, and protect yourself. Jesus reminds us that not every person we encounter is safe for us to be around: "Behold, I send you forth as sheep in the midst of wolves" [Matthew 10:16]. There will be people whose behavior and/or intentions are quite wolf-like, and we'll waste too much energy wishing they were different.

But let us not forget that God wants to change our hearts and perspectives, too.

Let's be real: surely there have been times when you've grumbled and felt low-key annoyed when God has nudged you to do some of the good works He has for you to do. Can you imagine how much darker the world would be if we shined our lights and did kind, beautiful things only when we felt amazing and ready?

Welcome those Godly nudges even on days when you feel kind of *meh*, my dear firefly.

The more we follow His lead and get to know the people around us, the more we will see them through His eyes – with compassion, empathy, sensitivity, and lovingkindness. As we slow down and really *look* at our coworkers (and our customers, clients, patients, students, and whomever we serve at our jobs), we may see human beings who need someone to shine a little light into their lives – especially on the days when they're being the worst version of themselves.

Hopefully, someone else will do that for us, too – on those rare (*ahem!*) days (*or weeks. . .or years. . .*) when we're not being the best version of ourselves. Honestly, who is at their best all the time?

Keep your eyes open, your mind in the present, and your heart sensitive enough to notice when someone in your workplace needs a bit of kindness – and offer it to that person. Be the one who buys the "Get Well Soon" card for that coworker who just had surgery. Be the one who checks on that other coworker who seems especially sad and distracted today. Be the one who stops and offers jumper cables even though you'd rather be at home eating gelato or fudge pops.

Maybe you don't see that person as your friend *(yet?)(okay, maybe not ever)*, but you and that person both have the same Someone pursing you – His name is Jesus. He wants a relationship with them. He wants a relationship with you, too. His unconditional love for each of us does not mean He approves of everything we do – such as when we don't treat the people around us right or when they aren't treating us right. But hopefully, people can tell who your Father is by the love you give.

And He instructs us to not hide our light from a world that needs it [Matthew 5:14-16].

There is always good work to be done.

FYI

"He that getteth wisdom loveth his own soul: he that keepeth understanding shall find good."

Proverbs 19:8 (KJV)

First and foremost, we must each learn the truth about who God is and about our own identities in Christ. In this way, we don't rely on the world to tell us who we are nor who we "should" be. There is no greater and more important truth than what we see in Jesus' life and in His Resurrection *(look to John 3:16)*.

In the workplace, we need to be willing to not only be accountable but encourage accountability within our business dealings. We do this by being knowledgeable about the companies where we work.

Pop quiz: What's your organization's attendance policy? What's the policy on being late to work? If you're able to earn paid time off (PTO) at your job, how many hours do you have? What are the guidelines regarding the dress code, overtime, and how to report misconduct?

Do you have (or know where to find) a copy of your organization's policy handbook?

In any workplace you're in, especially in a toxic one, it's crucial to know 1) Guidelines set out in the employee manual, 2) Job expectations and metrics (How is a "job well done" achieved for your role? Is there a probationary period for your position? How are company policy violations handled formally?), and 3) Company contact information (such as how to contact Human Resources, whether there is a tip line to report ethics concerns, etc.).

If your job is being a student at a college or university, always keep track of financial aid deadlines, make sure that you keep a copy of your plan of study that shows which courses have been completed and what's left to take (bonus points if it is signed by your academic advisor), and learn about FERPA (the Federal Educational Rights and Privacy Act). Get to know people in Student Services and find out about free resources available to you on campus, including tutoring and counseling.

You don't need to memorize all this info. What's most important is knowing *where* to go and how to obtain the information.

Knowing the rules, guidelines, and established outcomes involving different on-the-job scenarios prepares you for being an advocate for others and for yourself.

Advocacy is a skill I wish was taught more often in high schools and in higher education settings. We can learn how to better advocate for ourselves and how to advocate for others (while helping them to do so as well). Speaking up for myself is a skill I didn't have when I worked in toxic workplaces.

When we are asked or told to do something that is harmful or unsafe, violates personal or moral boundaries, or is ethically wrong, we can choose to speak up. We don't have to shout or scream – the truth would still be the truth even if you whispered it and even if your voice shakes nervously when you say it. Proverbs 31:9 reminds each of us to "open thy mouth, judge righteously, and plead the cause of the poor and needy."

We ask questions. We offer constructive feedback. We learn how to handle and receive constructive feedback. If there is anything that we don't understand – such as a policy, a process, an upcoming change, or the details about an insurance plan – we seek understanding and clarification from the people in our company who possess the knowledge *(we don't just post our questions and concerns to online discussion boards, turning the internet into our unofficial human resources department)(not that I've ever done that before. . .).*

If we are in a workplace that encourages dishonesty, we make an important decision about the kind of person we want to be – personally, I want to be at peace with the decisions I make during my shift. If I become the top earner at my company, but I had to lie, cheat, mislead other people, and abandon personal accountability to get there, what good is that? As Matthew 26:16 states, "For what is a man profited, if he shall gain the whole world, and lose his own soul? Or what shall a man give in exchange for his soul?"

Within Acts, we see the Apostle Paul advocate for himself and for his companions.

While in Philippi, Paul set an enslaved girl free from the evil spirit within her [Acts 16:16-24]. She was a fortune-teller, and the ones who had control over her and treated her as property made lots of money off her. Once she was set free, she was no longer a moneymaker for them.

An angry mob formed as a result – led by the men who had lost control of the enslaved girl, and then Paul and a fellow missionary named Silas were beaten and arrested. They spent the night in prison – praising God and leading prisoners as well as the jailer (and his household) to Christ.

The next morning, the magistrates of Philippi sent word to the jailer to set Paul and Silas free.

However, Paul responded, "They have beaten us openly uncondemned, being Romans, and have cast us into prison; and now do they thrust us out privily? nay verily; but let them come themselves and fetch us out" [Acts 16:37].

He was unwilling to accept being mistreated and then quietly sent away without holding people in power accountable for their actions, especially when they broke the law.

After he was arrested and beaten in Acts 22:24-29, Paul asked – fully knowing the answer, "Is it lawful for you to scourge a man that is a Roman, and uncondemned?" The chief captain in charge of his imprisonment was *shook* when the guard told him what Paul had asked. Paul was simply pointing out the truth: what was done to him was not only wrong, but illegal.

We become better at advocacy in the workplace by 1) Getting to know our identity, our worth, and who we are in Christ through a relationship with Him and by reading the Word, 2) Learning our organization's policies and procedures, 3) Obtaining general knowledge about employment laws such as the Family and Medical Leave Act (FMLA), the Occupational Health and Safety Act, and the Age Discrimination in Employment Act of 1967, and 4) Practicing and maintaining healthy boundaries both inside and outside our places of employment. We learn how to say *No, thank you* (or simply *No*) when we need to say it. We also learn who will be receptive to listening to us when there's a problem – and not forfeiting our peace by continuing to try to discuss issues with someone who routinely acts like a brick wall (see the devotion called *This Isn't Working*).

One side effect of being someone who embraces advocacy, through open communication, is that we give other people more grace.

Instead of expecting them to guess what we feel, what we need, or why we reacted in a certain way, we tell them. Instead of responding with the silent treatment or a starting a shouting match when someone offends us (and if we feel unable to move past it, even after praying about it), we have a conversation with the other person (if we feel safe to do so). As the Bible instructs us in Matthew 5:23-24, we are meant to try to work it out and heal the connection or relationship (if possible) so that when we worship, we don't carry the heavy weight of grudges, anger, misunderstandings, or unforgiveness. We'll be able to fully give our hearts to God when we worship instead of being distracted by what someone else has said or done (or what we've said and done).

We also learn how to apologize when we're the somebody who's done somebody wrong.

I think it's important to mention that advocacy is not about getting everything we want nor is it about controlling others. It's not about vengeance – that's up to God [Romans 12:19]. It's not about requiring people to see things as we see them. It's about communicating – instead of getting upset when people can't read our minds or guess what we need. It's about asking for resources – resources that are oftentimes available as per the law, especially if we have a disability – that will help us to do our jobs. Advocacy also means asking for help when we need it. It's about proactively finding out what resources are available to you. It's about holding a company accountable to its own policies and guidelines, especially ones regarding fairness, trustworthiness, and ethics.

We trust God to give us the courage to open our mouths and speak up. The Bible reassures us that Jesus is our ultimate Advocate pleading on our behalf: "Who is he that condemneth? It is Christ that died, yea rather, that is risen again, who is even at the right hand of God, who also maketh intercession for us" [Romans 8:34].

There are times when He gives me the courage and the words to speak up for myself – and then there are other instances when I must ask Him to be the One advocating for me – as I cling to Him quietly and let Him handle it. Either way, I need Him. Either way, I am not facing any situation alone because Christ is with me.

Gain knowledge about your workplace – its rules, policies, and procedures. Find out what resources are available to you at your organization and in your community. Sometimes, I will ask God for provision – and He will help me to realize that what I'm asking for is already available, I'm just overlooking it.

Speak up, and look around to see all that's possible, my friend. And never forget that even on your quieter days, you have an Advocate who is actively looking out for you.

This Isn't Working

"And I will give you a new heart, and I will put a new spirit in you. I will take out your stony, stubborn heart and give you a tender, responsive heart."

Ezekiel 36:26-27 (NLT)

If you told me that your workplace is dysfunctional, I'd ask you to tell me about the quality of communication at your organization. Effective communication within a business – between colleagues, and between supervisors and the ones they supervise – is part of the foundation for a healthy work environment. Unfortunately, the need to improve how we communicate is often neglected and treated as least important.

Have you ever tried to discuss problems with someone who was like a brick wall? It feels like every word you say just bounces off them. Or you get the feeling that the person isn't listening. I once became involved in a debate (i.e. an argument) with a coworker named Kevin who had previously asserted that he didn't have emotional walls – only boundaries. Well, it turned out that *he* was a wall. Anytime someone tried to teach Kevin something new and necessary at work, he mentally shut down. Anytime someone offered gentle correction and constructive comments, he chose instead to cling to his way of doing things. Kevin was part of a team, but he would rarely ask for help – even when he truly needed it.

Now, there are two twists to this story about this argument – *ahem,* debate – with my coworker Kevin. The first twist is that Kevin is actually one of my favorite people. Random fact: he'd never seen snow in person, but he really wanted to see it. He's kind and decent overall – but he's also incredibly stubborn. Our debate/argument lasted two rounds, and afterwards, I was so upset over feeling not heard and not understood by him – I decided to just keep my distance from Kevin.

I did not know one shouldn't bring up issues with him, but I learned soon enough that it was pointless and would end with me feeling even more stressed out.

One day after the disagreement, our wonderful southern city welcomed its first dusting of snow. And even though I was still hurt, frustrated, and angry over the interaction we'd had, a sudden jolt of joy hit me because somewhere in our community, Kevin was finally seeing snow for the first time in person.

This joy on his behalf confused me. Could I really be happy for someone whom I'd just had a horrible argument with? Could I actually be elated for someone whose stubbornness had helped me to feel unseen and unheard? Could I experience negative conflict with someone with seemingly no resolution in sight (*except to avoid one another indefinitely*) – and still want him to get the chance to build a very short snowman with the scarce amount of snow Alabama gets per winter?

Yes. Yes, I could.

After that moment of joy, I wondered curiously within myself, *Is this the kind of love Jesus was talking about? The kind of love where people can disagree with us, argue with us, shut us out, shut us down, misunderstand us, be misunderstood by us, get a peek at our insecurities and inner struggles, be given a peek at their insecurities and inner struggles, bump up against each other's differences – and yet, we still want to see the other person whole, happy, healed, joyful, safe, and welcomed into a loving community?*

I told you there were two twists to this story. The second twist is that what we argued about for two days wasn't even that important. Actually, how we communicate and how we disagree with someone is oftentimes more important than what we're arguing about. Conflict isn't inherently bad; it's how we handle it and what happens afterwards that matters.

Let's talk about better ways to approach disagreements in the workplace – especially when dealing with people who act like brick walls:

1. *Pause.* **Think it over before you bring up an issue with someone else.** Right after the incident happens, I know you really want to just keep it real and go talk it out immediately with the person who may have wronged you, but *just don't do it.* As Proverbs 14:29 states, "He that is slow to wrath is of great understanding: but he that is hasty of spirit exalteth folly." Talk to God about it first. Pray for Him to give you the ability to see the situation as it truly is – not just through a filter of hurt feelings. Check in with yourself: can you move past what happened or does it need to be addressed? If there's someone in your life who will give you honest feedback (instead of only people who will tell us that we're absolutely right even when we aren't), tell them what happened so they can help you gain further perspective.

2. **Approach the person and address the problem (if necessary).** You've prayed, you had a little snackie snack, you drank some water (*stay hydrated, my friend*), and you thought through what happened as well as talked to someone wise and objective about it. You no longer want to angrily throw office supplies at a wall. However, you realize that the issue still needs to be discussed with the other person. When speaking to them, keep your voice level and calm. State the issue, briefly explain why you needed to bring it up/include your point of view regarding what happened, ask their perspective on it (this gives them a chance to explain their side of it). Did the person offer solutions? Did you offer solutions? Is a compromise needed?

3. **You've approached the person, but he didn't seem receptive to what you said. This isn't working.** Here's where you persist and argue your point of view until the other person gives in. JUST KIDDING. Don't do that, seriously. Please remember that many people shut down during confrontations, disagreements, or even when there's the faintest whiff of constructive criticism in the air (*hint: constructive criticism smells like fresh cilantro – some folks can take the scent, others would rather live without it*). They may not be able to mentally process nor take in what you're saying right in that moment, so it will appear as if you're not being heard nor understood. You may not get the reactions or responses that you expect. Once the discussion is over, evaluate how you handled it: Did you listen to their perspective? Did you avoid leading with anger? Did you approach them in the best way possible or do you think a different communication style might

have been better (example: Some people prefer you to be direct and blunt while someone else might require a gentler approach)? Did you apologize, if necessary, for any aspect of the initial conflict that happened due to your own actions or words?

4. **Possible Outcome A: After you've discussed the problem, the person didn't change his behavior nor work to improve the issue.** Time passes by, and you see that the person truly wasn't receptive to what you said. The original problem gets worse (the person may deny there's even a problem that needs to be fixed). You may feel upset, angry, and frustrated all over again – and ready to have another discussion about the same issue. Sure, you could hash it out once more with the person using a different approach. Let's say you do, but there's even worse pushback and refusal to listen than before.

Remember how you prayed to God, asking Him to show you how things truly are? We can pray that for the other person, too. Maybe you can't get through to the person, but God can. Another option is to point out the problem to someone else who can fix it – such as Human Resources, a supervisor, an anonymous workplace tipline, or an employee advocate. Lastly, you can also let the tree bear its fruit [Matthew 7:17-20]. Unfortunately, you may not be the only one who struggles to communicate with the person. It may take time – and more disagreements with other people – before your coworker acknowledges their own role in the conflicts. It make take for the problem to grow massive before the person thinks, *All right, I really need to do something about this.*

5. **Possible Outcome B: After you've discussed the problem, the person changed his behavior and is doing his best to fix the issue.** Times passes by. Maybe you didn't think the person heard nor understood you, but you see through their actions that he *actually did* hear you and that he cares about your perspective. He just needed time after the argument to process what you said. Yes, maybe an emotional, protective wall went up within him during the disagreement, but when he was alone and felt safe enough to do so, he lowered the wall and considered his role in the problem.

6. **Embrace the awkward.** I've learned from experience that when you talk it out with someone or bring up a problem, a period of awkwardness may ensue after the conversation. That's okay. Eventually, the awkwardness clears away with time. Think of the act of bringing up a problem or issue with someone like stretching a rubber band. If you use harsh words, the rubber band will get stretched too much and might pop. But if you are direct yet still considerate of the other person when addressing the problem, the rubber band will stretch and stretch just enough due to being pulled in different directions at the same time. It doesn't pop and isn't ruined. Afterwards, the awkwardness comes as you stop pulling at the rubber band and it snaps back into shape. Give the rubber band time to regain its shape as the tension dies down – and embrace the awkwardness between you and the other person, if there is any.

Nowadays, it's harder to ask people how they may be personally contributing to a miserable, unhealthy, or unproductive situation in their lives because pop culture leads us to label all disagreements and interactions with personalities that clash with our own as a shade of gaslighting. There is a difference between the suggestion to self-reflect, incidents when people disagree with our viewpoints, or times when we need to take personal accountability versus gaslighting. Gaslighting is a toxic, manipulative, dangerous behavior by which someone routinely invalidates what you know about yourself, your identity, your feelings, and your beliefs. It intentionally causes confusion, pain, and self-doubt. It poisons and destroys your mental health.

Self-reflection and prayer, on the other hand, clear away confusion. Both reaffirm who we are, what we know, and our connection to our faith. God loves us, and He will correct us when we need it because of His love for us. No, you aren't responsible for how someone else chooses to treat you – that's not within your control. Shift your focus. I can tell you honestly that there were times when my own insecurities cheered me on as I hastily jumped into tiresome, unnecessary arguments. Afterward, I felt that still, small voice inside gently telling me why I acted the way I did, that I'm still loved, and that I needed to apologize.

As the key verse says, sometimes it's *my* heart that is stony and stubborn. But God.

When we clash with someone (such as a coworker), can we pause, slow down, and think before we say another word? Can we give others time to process what was said and time to make things better? Can we say we're sorry when we are the ones who get it wrong?

By the way, my coworker Kevin is still one of my favorite people. He's the one who taught me that you can slow down and ask for time to process what's happening *during* an argument (*y'all, be patient with me; I know I should know this by now, but I didn't*). Our argument – and its sequel, which happened the next day – actually strengthened our working relationship because we were both willing to do better afterward. I learned, through this conflict, that you can still want all the good things for someone even when you're so angry with them that you temporarily can't stand their face.

(Was that too honest? Can I write that in a devotional?)

And if you have a choice between an argument and a snowball fight? Always choose snowball fight.

(Bonus twist to the story: That particular argument with Kevin, which could have been a short, calm conversation if I'd followed the steps listed above: I was the one who was wrong. Ooomph.)

Not This Again

"Be strong and of a good courage, fear not, nor be afraid of them: for the Lord thy God, He it is that doth go with thee; He will not fail thee, nor forsake thee."

Deuteronomy 31:6 (KJV)

How do you start and end your day?

On my worst days as an employee in toxic environments, I played the same songs (in my mind) every morning before getting ready for my shift that day. Here are the titles of my AM playlist:

- "Lord, Not This Again"
- "If I Caught the Bubonic Plague in the Next Five Minutes, I Wouldn't Have to Go to Work, Right?"
- "Lord, I Don't Think I Can Do This Again"
- "Today's Going to be a Terrible Day"
- "I Need This Job. I'll Never Find a Better One. I Need to Just Grin and Bear It"

As soon as my eyes opened and before I raised my head from my pillow, the usual dread, fear, and anxiety would flood me.

Before I'd go to sleep at night (*if I was able to sleep*), I'd replay the unkind communication happening in the office. I meditated on how a certain coworker – despite having his own work to do – would spend his downtime looking for any mistake I'd made, and if he found one, he'd happily rush to point it out to my boss every time (and offer me a smug, self-satisfied smile). I'd recall the conversations about me that my boss would have with another coworker in her office. Sometimes, they'd close the door, and sometimes, they'd leave it open (either way, I could always hear their unkind words and their laughter). Some of their favorite topics: my body, my hair, the way I talk, and what I'd done wrong.

Even worse was the disrespectful way they'd talk about some of the people we were there to serve.

I thought about how the people in my workplace always excluded me from lunches that included everyone else in the department. The worst part of that was how important information regarding our department was often discussed during these lunches, so I'd be the last person to know anything. And how my boss would treat me like I was the most unintelligent creature she'd ever encountered every time I asked a question, so I became afraid of asking for help or additional training.

There were days when my coworkers would barely speak to each other. There were times when I listened to one of them screaming angrily during phone calls.

This position – before I started working there – looked like my dream job. It came with my own office, a good salary, benefits, and was at a respected organization. In my mind, this was the best job I'd *ever* have. I felt lucky for being chosen for the position. Every new employee had to pass a probationary period, and I feared that if I talked about the bad treatment, they wouldn't allow me to stay past probation.

Plus, I'd never learned how to speak up for myself – or that I had a right to do so.

When we believe that something or someone that is hurting us mentally, physically, emotionally, and/or spiritually is the best option we'll ever have, then we need to take a step back and reevaluate our perspective. When we'd rather catch the Bubonic Plague than go to work, that's probably a sign that workplace has at least a *wee bit* of toxicity in it (*and/or* the job is not a good fit for us).

Difficult workplaces rife with dysfunctional communication tend to shift my manageable anxiety into unmanageable territory. My first thoughts in the morning were anxious and depressed ones about my job, and my last thoughts at night were self-loathing ones fueled by the words said over me while I was at work. When you're working a job that causes you high levels of stress, pain, and anxiety, but despite that, you're afraid of losing it – that's such a conflicted way to live! I'm sorry if you're currently living this out. I know what it's like.

Notice how I mentioned that I felt *lucky* to have been chosen for that job. If we're not careful, we can slip into a mindset in which we believe that being chosen is solely about our own efforts, about luck, or because of our own goodness. There are two problems with this way of thinking: 1) If we believe that being chosen in life is 100% based on always getting things right without any mistakes, our own perfect timing, how people feel about us, and other superficial reasons, then that means the same people who choose us can also reject us and decide the trajectory of our lives (*also, so-called "luck" will fail you*), and 2) We might start to believe that God is the same way – that He chose us but will just as easily dismiss or cancel us if we mess up.

This is not truth. God did not choose us based on luck nor based on what we do or don't do. He *did not* choose us because we're pretty, charismatic, have perfectionist tendencies, or because of who our parents are.

He chose us because of who He is. He chose us because He wanted us. He chose to love us. He chose us as His own. And the Bible says that Jesus is the same yesterday, today, and forever [Hebrews 13:8], so none of that is changing.

What heavy thoughts are living rent-free with a move-in special and water included in your mind?

Those first minutes after we wake up are powerful. We cannot begin the day already in a hope-and-joy deficit. And I know you said you'd stop and get gas before work, but let's refill those hope, joy, and faith tanks within you in the morning, too.

Honestly, it's not fair for Monday and its troubles to stick around into Tuesday, serving you a breakfast of day-old, cold coffee, and a microwaved Hot Pocket that's still cold in the middle.

It's like dealing with that friend or relative who never finishes a phone call with you. Five minutes into the call, he always says, "Hey, let me call you back. . ."

Sometimes, he *does* call back. Then ten minutes into this second call, you get hit with a "Hey, Scooter's calling. I've got to take this. I'll call you right back."

We can't allow yesterday and all its problems to keep calling us back. You've got stuff to do. Even if it's resting – *resting* is stuff that needs to be done.

The key verse is one to remember when you need encouragement to start your day: God is always with you. He's got you. When we wake up (and throughout the day), it's important to add thoughts that renew us, encourage us, and build us up. I said *add* because I know how hard it is to try to stop anxious thoughts altogether.

Instead, when we are bombarded by those thoughts of defeat, fear, anxiety, and scarcity, we add a thought that challenges those thoughts. And I don't just think the hopeful thoughts – I say them out loud.

Here is my new playlist:

- "Let everything that hath breath praise the Lord" [Psalm 150:6] and let everything that praises the Lord, have breath. *(I also say that second part as a reminder to myself to breathe deeply, which helps to calm me. Our lungs need more than shallow breaths.)*

- "But as for me and my house, we will serve the Lord" [Joshua 24:15]. *(I usually say I instead of we and tap the side of my head. This is to remind myself that I don't serve my anxiety, I serve God and I trust in what He says about me and my future.)*

- "Now faith is the substance of things hoped for, the evidence of things not seen" [Hebrews 11:1]. *(My God is a God of abundance. I don't live according to scarcity nor according to what it looks like. My faith is in God's active power and grace at work in my life.]*

What are your first thoughts in the morning? Is your mind usually filled with worries about yesterday or the day ahead? Before you begin your morning routine, are you able to pause long enough to add thoughts of God's truth, thanksgiving and gratefulness, victory, hope, encouragement, and love (toward God, toward others, and towards yourself) to your mental playlist? Will you start saying kind and loving things to yourself – *about yourself* – even before you raise your head from your pillow?

Can you choose a verse from the Bible that you can speak over your day before you get out of bed?

I've found it helpful to play worship music as I get dressed, take time to read God's Word before I leave to go to work, and write in a journal.

While you speak life over yourself (*yay!*), I'll head into the kitchen and make you some breakfast tots because you're a winner, and winners get tater tots.

Coping with Change Fatigue

(*or* Whose Idea was *THIS*?)

"God is our refuge and strength, a very present help in trouble. Therefore will not we fear, though the earth be removed, and though the mountains be carried into the midst of the sea; Though the waters thereof roar and be troubled, though the mountains shake with the swelling thereof. Selah."

Psalm 46:1-3 (KJV)

You may have heard of change fatigue (also known as change burnout or change exhaustion). In general, this is a sense of powerlessness, frustration, discouragement, and tiredness caused by being hit by change after change (or one massive change) – while not being given enough support and time to adjust to the changes. Change burnout is not necessarily about your unwillingness or inability to adapt to change; rather, it is built on an unrealistic expectation for people to just keep *going and going and going* without taking a moment to process what's happening around them or to them.

Constant unexpected changes take a lot of mental and emotional energy to cope with – so as a way of dealing with change, some employees switch from being engaged to being passive and apathetic in the workplace (perhaps even "quietly quitting"), others lose respect for their company's leadership and the company itself, and the work environment may become weighed down by discontentment, fear of the unknown, and demotivation.

Employees may not totally understand what's changing – *and why*, even though the change affects them. In the workplace, change often feels personal. Due to poor communication between leadership and the rest of the team, employees may feel unsupported, unprepared, and devalued when required to silently adjust over and over again.

Throughout my career, there have been times when the top leadership at past organizations set into motion a series of changes (or one big change that carried a lot of weight) – and in response to those changes, I thought, *It feels like this company does not value nor care about its employees* or *It's obvious that this change was thought up by someone who has never worked a week doing what my team does on a daily basis* or simply, *Who in the world thought this was a good idea?*

For some people, constant changes feel invigorating. For me and others, it feels chaotic and unstable – and I need time to catch my breath and cope with it all. Both perspectives are valid.

Here are seven suggestions for coping with change in the workplace (*before* it becomes change fatigue):

1. **Remember that God will be your Rock – and He won't be shaken, moved, nor changed.** The key verse for this devotion reminds us that even when the circumstances around us become unstable, confusing, and chaotic, He will be our strength and stick with us through whatever comes our way. Psalm 40:2 states that God sees when we feel like the rug has been pulled from under us or when we're in sticky situations – and He sets us on

steady, solid ground. Two of the most important constants in your life are God's love for you and His presence.

2. **Change something you can change.** Maybe your workplace is going through restructuring or other uncomfortable changes. It may seem like you receive an email every other day about a new policy or rule that directly impacts how you perform your job. Let's turn our attention from that right now – and consider other areas of your life. Is there something you've always wanted to change up in your home, but you never seem to get around to doing it? Maybe you have a closet (or a whole garage) that needs cleaning out, or maybe you've always wanted to make your living room more *hygge* (that's fancy-talk for *super comfy*). Or maybe there's a class you've always wanted to take, or you feel a nudge to put more time into turning acquaintances into friendships. Maybe it's time to get more involved in small groups at church. You can also try something new like that café you keep driving past on the way to work. Perhaps you have little or no say regarding the changes at work, but you can launch your own potentially wonderful and fulfilling changes in the rest of your life.

3. **Take time to pause. Get away to your wilderness.** Notice the word *Selah* in the key verse for this devotion. The meaning of this word is often debated, but some scholars believe that it indicates a pause (Soroski, 2018). That pause, that Selah at the end of the key verse is asking you to really take in the words you just read. Even if your world goes through total upheaval, God is

with you. Building on this, sometimes we need to take a break and get away from our situation, even for just a little while. Jesus modeled this whenever He would walk away from the crowd and take some time in the wilderness to pray. Where do you go when you need a moment to breathe, reflect, refresh, and be alone with God? Getting away for a little while can also give our minds the time to adapt to changes happening mentally and emotionally at work *(refer to the devotion titled "Stress & Rest" for more on this)*.

4. **Make a list of the things you'd like to accomplish in the short-term and long-term and/or a list of what (and who) matters to you.** What are the goals you'd like to achieve beyond your current workplace? All goals welcome! Mine range from becoming a better steward over my finances to crocheting an entire blanket from start to finish (with discounted, soft, sparkly yarn – of course). Think of what you value outside of your workplace. One thing I'm thankful for is how God has given me meaningful, fulfilling friendships with wonderful female friends – and these friends continue to help me grow. Therefore, two aspects of my life that I value are personal growth and supportive connection with others. Now, imagine a seesaw – then mentally place your goals, cherished memories, hopes for the future, thoughts of the people and pets you love, and your values on one seat, and place the changes at work on the other seat. What matters the most – and thus, weighs the most? How much do the current changes at your present workplace affect the trajectory of your life? Are those changes worth worrying about?

5. **Change someone else's life – for the better.** You have the potential to make someone's day go from *meh* to unexpectedly good. Acts of kindness (big and small) can help change the perspective of a stranger, acquaintance, coworker, friend, or family member. I know this is true because people have helped me greatly by offering me a hug, by giving me a compliment or encouraging words, or by donating nonperishables to food banks I turned to when I couldn't afford meals.

6. **Recall good changes (because not all changes are terrible).** Listen, I'm one of those people who has trust issues when it comes to change. I tend to automatically assume that change will lead to pain and loss. But think of times when a change was good, and especially take a moment to remember changes that you thought would be bad but ended up leading to positive outcomes. Consider natural changes that occur around you. I live in the Southern USA, so I cheer for that shift from Sweaty Girl Summer to Cozy Girl Fall (*the humidity down here during the summer is no joke!*). God gives us beautiful change as witnessed via the seasons or even sunsets and sunrises. Lastly, remember you've overcome unwanted or unexpected changes before – and you'll overcome the current ones, too.

7. **If you're in leadership, be sure to communicate, empathize, and listen to your team when they express themselves.** For many people, just being able to talk openly about what's happening helps them to adapt, accept, and adjust to workplace changes. Explain the intentions behind the adjustments, be clear

about who and what is affected, and emphasize how much you appreciate your team and the work they do. Encourage employees as they put the changes into action. Verbalize how you understand their uncertainty, confusion, and frustration. Even if you're only following directives from the corporate or regional office, you have the power to help employees ease into and cope with changes.

Every workplace will come with changes – some you'll like, and some you won't. I don't say this to minimize how you feel, especially if you're struggling (remember, my own first reaction to change is *No, thanks!*). Instead, I'm reminding both of us to adjust our perspective: the changes happening at your job today likely won't bother you as much (or at all) months from now. If it's your hope to do so, you may be at an entirely different workplace altogether in a year or so.

What truly matters? What holds the most weight in your life? What deserves most of your energy and attention?

Give it time. Wait and see. Never forget that we can remain on solid ground (mentally and emotionally) – even when the world around us feels unsteady and unpredictable.

And if those changes prove themselves to actually be not-so-great, maybe they will be phased out like Crystal Pepsi, Taco Bell's seafood salad, and my questionable choice to wear orange socks with sandals in high school.

(Crystal Pepsi was kind of awesome, by the way).

Gossip in the Workplace

"And as ye would that men should do to you, do ye also to them likewise."

Luke 6:31 (KJV)

Two things that can bring coworkers together are complaining and negative gossip. Negative gossip is what I call an unhealthy bonding technique – *bad bonding* – because it does indeed foster connection between individuals or within a group, but it's often done at the expense of someone else (we'll cover complaining in the next devotion). At the heart of workplace gossip is a desire to build relationships with our coworkers.

It is part of human nature to want to know what's going on in your environment by sharing and seeking information. Surprisingly, gossip can be classified as positive, neutral, or negative, but negative gossip occurs the most often (Miller, 2019).

We're here to chit-chat about negative gossip – the type that involves unkind, harmful discussion about other people's personal business. Even though this devotion is listed under the *Dysfunctional Workplace* category, harmful gossip happens even in fantastic workplaces.

Here in the Southern USA, we may start our bit of gossip with a phrase like "Now, you know I love everybody, and I would never say anything bad about anyone, *but* let me tell you about what Jack did. . ." or "Bless her heart – wait until I tell you what I heard about Janet. . ."

To be honest with you, I've let myself get swept up into harmful gossip in the workplace. I listened to it, and then I recounted what I heard to others. This was back when I didn't understand how damaging it could be. I believed that sharing and listening to pernicious gossip was just what people do, that's just how people communicate, and if everyone else is gossiping, who am I to not join in? Whenever a coworker pulled me aside into our own little bubble, and confidentially told me about someone else's private life, I felt the sense of connection that I longed for so much.

Someone trusted me enough to confide in me. Except it was about someone else's personal stuff. Was this really the kind of closeness and intimacy that I wanted?

God wouldn't allow me to stay in that little bubble of idle chatter. As I drew closer to Him and my relationship with Him deepened, He led me to see the destruction – to others and to myself – that was caused by harmful gossip.

Whenever I'd stick around and listen to any unkind stories about a coworker (instead of changing the subject or excusing myself from the conversation), whatever was said would stay with me. The Word talks about how we must be on guard to prevent a bitter root from growing within us or within our lives [Hebrews 12:15] – and gossip became a bitter root within me. After an especially terrible story that I was told about a coworker's divorce, I felt so horrible – about what my coworker had gone through *and* about knowing something so personal – that I couldn't sleep that night.

Would I want strangers and acquaintances knowing such private details about the most painful experiences in my life? I have gone through this – it feels isolating, humiliating, and painful. The key verse for this devotion reminds us of how to treat others. If we wouldn't want to endure the pain of our personal business being spread throughout the workplace, we also shouldn't put anyone else through that.

I've seen coworkers suffer professional repercussions due to unfounded rumors. There were fellow team members who had their mental health struggles made worse by mean-spirited gossip.

Even further, harmful gossiping or being known as the office gossip does not help us to build healthy, productive connections with our coworkers. As followers of Christ, we are called to love others, and one of the ways we show love is by listening to one another. For me, it is an honor whenever a coworker I've known for a while feels safe enough to tell me about an embarrassing experience, a personal struggle that is impacting their work, or their hopes for the future.

Perhaps you don't want to create close connections with your coworkers. I understand. Some people like to keep their personal lives totally separate from their work lives *(hmm, maybe one reason is to avoid being the topic of gossip?)*. Or you may be in leadership, and desire to maintain strict professional boundaries. Even if you prefer to not go out for lattes with your coworkers, there is another benefit (beyond forming friendships) of being a person who doesn't participate in negative gossip: your workplace culture boosts its levels of grace and trustworthiness among the staff. Can you imagine how much weight is lifted off employees' shoulders when they know that one of their work-related mistakes or the details of their performance reviews won't be the talk of the office?

Our willingness to routinely participate in negative gossip should lead us to check in with our own hearts. Why are we saying or repeating such unkind words? Are we being motivated by loneliness, jealousy, fear, hurt, or another unaddressed emotion? Whatever is going on within us eventually finds its way into our words. As Luke 6:45 states, "A good man out of the good treasure of his heart bringeth forth that which is good. . ."

Lastly, have you ever been having a decent (or wonderful) day at work, and then a coworker tells you something critical that another coworker said about you? Whenever this happened to me, it added unnecessary worry and stress – plus, I'd end up spending the rest of the workday being upset about this secondhand information. We don't need to know what everyone is saying about us in order to do our job. We don't need to know how everyone feels about us or what they think about us. As mentioned in another devotion, if someone is upset about something we've said or done – especially if we may not know that we've done something wrong, it is that person's responsibility to let us know that there is a problem (or a supervisor/Human Resources needs to address the issue with us). This goes back to not expecting people to guess how we feel. If someone wants to complain endlessly about us to others but never wants to talk to us about what's wrong nor seek a solution, then that person may believe the problem can't be fixed (so they cope by venting). Please understand, though, there will be times when a person doesn't feel safe or comfortable with addressing certain problems directly with us, but hopefully, they will discuss it with people in the workplace who can address the issue.

But if we know that we wronged someone else, we should take accountability and try to make amends.

The Bible tells us several times to avoid unkind idle chatter, and to instead choose words that build each other up. Completely avoiding uncharitable gossip may not be easy, so we should give ourselves grace if we slip back into this old habit. May God strengthen us and enable us to do better next time.

Have you ever participated in workplace gossip? What are some helpful strategies that you can use to deal with unkind gossip about coworkers?

Gripe Squad

"Death and life are in the power of the tongue: and they that love it shall eat the fruit thereof."

Proverbs 18:21 (KJV)

Have you ever gone out to lunch with your coworkers – and afterwards, you realized that all you and your work friends did was talk about work? Excuse me – I didn't mean to say *talked about work*. Let's try that again.

Have you ever gone out to lunch with your coworkers – and realized that all you and your work buddies did was *complain* about work? Like 80% or more of the conversation was a vent session while enjoying tacos and amazing guac.

When we have a bad day at work, a series of bad days at work, or if we work in a chronically stressful environment, it becomes second nature to spend our downtime recounting the latest workplace annoyances to anyone who will listen. Totally understandable – I've done it, too. In the past, I've tended to use either one of two approaches: 1) Kept what I was going through locked inside of me – perhaps thinking that if I didn't talk about what was wrong, it would somehow fix itself *(besides, I thought the reason I was struggling in a toxic environment was due to me not being "strong" enough),* or 2) Aired all my grievances as often as possible by complaining to coworkers and posting miserable status updates on social media.

My coworkers and I played the very best game: rant volleyball. We would gather, then we'd each take turns discussing something in our workplace that was endlessly frustrating, overwhelming, unnecessarily confusing, or unfair. After one person said her grievance, all the other coworkers would nod and agree with everything she'd said – and assure her that her grievance was indeed the most horrible thing to happen to anyone in existence. Then the next person would answer with his own grievance, and we'd agree with him – that what he'd said was indeed the most horrible thing to happen to anyone in existence.

We were very unofficially known as the Gripe Squad. You most likely have an unofficial Gripe Squad in your workplace.

I called our venting *rant volleyball*, but I suppose it was also like we were sewing a *patchwork complaint quilt*. Every time we spent all our time together – mostly complaining, we added squares to the big ole metaphorical complaint quilt. But the thing about metaphorical patchwork complaint quilts is, they will never keep you warm.

And you really can't win at rant volleyball. In fact, every time my coworkers and I came together to groan about work, I'd feel a little bit better, but usually, I'd feel incredibly tired, angry, and discouraged afterward. Even further, our Gripe Squad's identity was built on unhappiness. Grumbling was the glue that held us together. Our group identity was tied to bonding over complaining about our jobs – and rarely did anyone want to challenge that identity by adding a different perspective.

Let me say that it is important for us to open up. Please don't hold what you're going through within you – forcing yourself to live silently and secretly overwhelmed *(we'll discuss this in a later devotion)*. You can always bring all your pain and grievances to God, pour out your thoughts into a journal, and share what's going on in your life with friends, mentors, and/or a professional counselor.

However, we must be careful to avoid the trap of conversations weighed down by complaints. Complaining has a way of commanding the spotlight in our minds. We can become so accustomed to venting that we can slip into autopilot and build our entire perspective on only talking about what's wrong.

Strengthening interpersonal bonds with our coworkers can have personal and professional benefits. Communication is one way that we strengthen our connections with each other, and we should be able to discuss areas that need improvement in our workplaces so that we can seek solutions together.

Hence the problem with the Gripe Squad. So often, very little time is given to brainstorming solutions, seeing or seeking other people's points of view (such as encouraging a coworker to ask his supervisor directly about the reasoning behind a recent – and frustrating – departmental decision), nor do we spend a big enough chunk of the conversation encouraging each other. We could also use our time together to learn more positive, fun information about the people we work with – instead of giving all your energy to talking about how the Breakroom Bandit always eats your homemade lunches, even though your name is clearly written on them.

Yes, we should be able to open up and have honest conversations, but our conversations also need to be balanced. The key verse reminds us of the power that our words can have. Our words can either speak death, discouragement, and hopelessness over our situations or our words can speak life, renewal, encouragement, and hope over our lives.

So often, we just need to be heard. You don't need to totally eliminate talking about your bad day. However, maybe you and your coworkers can try setting a time limit for how long your venting sessions can last – and when the time is up, you all collectively shift the conversation to different topics. Or you can decide that the next time you all get together for coffee, you won't talk about work at all – especially since your Gripe Squad took home the championship last week with the amount of ranting done over Boba tea.

And if you're not sure what to talk about that isn't work-related, you can always talk about air fryers. People really love talking about their air fryers.

Say *Hello* to Them, Anyway

"We love Him, because He first loved us."

1 John 4:19 (KJV)

"Hello, Jamie!"

My cheerful greeting – paired with a smile – was always met with averted eyes and silence. Jamie would walk right past me every time without saying a word or even acknowledging my presence.

At the beginning of each shift, I said *Hello* with a smile. During the shift, I'd ask Jamie questions – but he wouldn't respond. He wouldn't even look me in the eyes. Eventually, I decided that Jamie didn't like me: maybe he wasn't a fan of morning people, or cheerful people, or people in general. Maybe he just didn't like the cut of my jib – as they said in olden times. I racked my brain, trying to pinpoint any way I may have offended him in the past – but I couldn't think of anything.

Still, day after day, week after week, I cheerfully greeted him even though he never said a word.

Months passed like that, and during a meeting, his supervisor happened to mention that Jamie struggles with extreme social anxiety. Talking to people and making eye contact is difficult for him. She was proud of him, though, because he was gradually becoming comfortable with customers and beginning to communicate more.

I'd made up my mind that Jamie didn't like me, but the truth was, Jamie's behavior wasn't about me. Fortunately, I had never stopped being nice to him. I never stopped joyfully saying *Hello* to him.

More time went by, and eventually, Jamie started offering me a mumbled, quiet *Hello* in response. Eventually, he would approach me and start short conversations. Gradually, I found out that Jamie told funny jokes.

I've worked with other coworkers who would ignore me when I spoke, roll their eyes at me when I asked them questions, or give me cold stares when I smiled at them.

Still, whenever I interacted with any of them, I did what we talked about in a previous devotion: I shined my light. I maintained my joy and my kindness, even when I wanted to mirror their reactions and ignore them right back.

Why should we change who we are and stop doing what we believe is right because of someone else's behavior?

As followers of Christ, we are called to act in ways that may confuse the world – especially in the way that we love other people. Our aim, of course, isn't to do things differently solely for the sake of being different or special; rather, our central focus is our relationship with God. Our second focus is on our relationships with our fellow humans, including our coworkers and supervisors.

There was one week when two of my coworkers seemed to be at odds with each other. When I took them aside separately and asked them what was happening, each of them said that they had no idea why the other person was angry with them. Imagine two people not communicating because they each assume that the other person dislikes them – when the truth was that one of them was just less talkative lately because they were coping with personal problems, and the other person responded to the first employee's withdrawn behavior with the silent treatment and avoidance.

How often do we find ourselves waiting for someone to talk to us first? Waiting for someone to reach out and try to get to know us?

Why are we waiting? The key verse reminds us that God didn't wait for us to love Him *before* He decided to love us. Instead, He chooses to love us first. Yes, us – you, and me, and the coworker who takes your parking spot every day, and the coworker who gossips about you, and the boss who is always short on patience, and the customers who say the most unkind things. He loves us even before we become shinier, more well-adjusted people. God showed us that love is not something we earn by being perfect, likable, or experts at adulting. Even though we humans can be difficult, grumpy, hangry, short-tempered, withdrawn, dismissive, hypocritical, judgmental, argumentative, angry, rude, unforgiving, and slow to love other people, God still loved us all so, so much that He sent his only Son – Jesus Christ – to rescue us through the crucifixion and the Resurrection [John 3:16; Romans 5:8].

Some of us grew up guessing other people's emotions by reading into how they communicate nonverbally. Or maybe it came from past relationships or other interactions in your adult years. We learned to pay close attention to body language, especially facial expressions, and when the people around us looked upset, our minds may have assumed that any of their unwanted emotions were our fault. Even further, we might have made it our responsibility to "fix" the feelings of the folks around us.

Unfortunately, routinely guessing how someone else feels – and assuming that our guesses are always 100% correct – may be a survival skill that we carry into our workplaces. The problem is that we don't guess correctly all the time (maybe not even most of the time), and we may adjust our own behavior based on incomplete or incorrect assumptions. We may also assume that we still need to fix other people's feelings (we don't need to) or we may project our own feelings onto our coworkers. 1 Corinthians 2:11 reminds me that the only person who knows what's going on in my mind – my worries, my feelings, my thoughts – with certainty is me.

Same for each of our coworkers. Ditto for the other people in our lives.

And let's be real: sometimes, even *I* don't know the exact reason why I react or feel a certain way unless I spend time by myself, thinking it over.

We must avoid assuming that someone else's behavior – such as pulling away or being withdrawn – was caused by something we said or did. Instead, we can either A) Check in with the person, letting him know that we're available to talk if there's anything he wants to talk about – then we give him space, or B) We remain kind to the person but give her space – and we trust that she will come and talk to us about what's on her mind when she's ready to do so (if necessary – she may work through the issue herself).

As mentioned earlier, there will be times when we may want to treat people how they treat us, particularly when they treat us unkindly. However, do we really want to allow someone else's emotions or actions to dictate how we choose to feel and behave?

Our ability to be joyful is not chained to how anyone treats us. As Psalm 33:21 says, "For our heart shall rejoice in Him, because we have trusted in His holy name." We trust Christ to be the source of our joy.

Do you mind starting (or continuing) to be kind – even to the coworkers who aren't kind to you? This can be as simple as offering a smile, encouraging words, or even just a cheerful *Hello!* when you see them.

By the way, great job this week. You're doing so well.

Micromanagement & You

(*or* The Great Micromanagement Extravaganza)

"And let us not be weary in well doing: for in due season we shall reap, if we faint not."

Galatians 6:9 (KJV)

From past experiences and based on conversations with both supervisors and employees, I dare to say that most of the time (but not all the time) – micromanaging behavior is not about the employee.

However, employees often cite being constantly micromanaged as one of the top factors that make their workplaces unbearable. So why do managers, supervisors, and coworkers do it, anyway?

We'll talk about *why*, but first, let's briefly define it: micromanagement is when someone gives you a task to do but proceeds to either do all or most of the task for you – *or* the person insists that you complete the task as they watch, correct, and/or criticize you the entire time. A formal definition for micromanagement from the Cambridge Dictionary is "to control every part of a situation, project, etc., even including the small details, in a way that may not be necessary and may not give enough responsibility to other employees." A worker who experiences micromanagement may feel as if her knowledge, capabilities, experiences, and contributions are constantly being scrutinized or devalued.

Throughout the New Testament, we see multiple examples of Jesus having His ministry, identity, actions, and abilities challenged.

- Challenged by the disciples of John the Baptist about why Him and His disciples didn't fast like them [Luke 5:33-35].

- Challenged by His own disciples such as when a well-meaning Peter told Jesus that He wouldn't need to experience the Resurrection [Mark 8:31-33].

- Challenged by the people in His hometown when they were unable to see Him as more than the carpenter's son, so they refused to believe in Him [Luke 4:22-24].

- Challenged because His hometown was Nazareth. Nathanael – before he became His disciple – didn't believe that the Messiah could be from such a place as Nazareth because nothing good comes from there [John 1:46].

- Challenged by the Sadducees and the Pharisees many, many times – such as regarding His authority to forgive sins, heal people, perform other miracles, and expel people from the Temple who had turned God's house into a marketplace [Mark 11:15-28].

- Challenged by the people who came to Him for help like the father with the son who was tormented by an evil spirit that the disciples couldn't free him from. The doubtful father requested Jesus to heal his son – *if* He could [Mark 9:14-23].

- Challenged by the enemy of our faith: When Jesus was led into the wilderness for forty days, the enemy tried to cause Jesus to doubt His own identity as the Son of God [Luke 4:1-13].

Everything Jesus did was under scrutiny.

If you've ever dealt with constant criticism and nitpicking, you know how frustrating it can feel. I know what it's like to be treated as if you don't know how to do your job, even though you've been doing it well for a while.

Let's dive into the *why*. Here are some of the reasons why supervisors (and coworkers) micromanage in the workplace:

- **Unclear of What It Means to be a Supervisor:** Not everyone in a leadership role has been trained (or has extensive experience) with leading others. Many people hear the word *supervisor* and believe it simply means telling people what to do as well as exercising power over them. Of course, a huge aspect of being in a supervisory role is delegating tasks, but a supervisor must also be able to effectively train, motivate, and give space for employees to competently fulfill their job duties. Micromanagers may also lack the ability to give clear instructions and find it easier to just do the task themselves rather than learn how to explain what needs to be done. Even further, they may believe that supervisors are supposed to be cold, critical, and impersonal.

- **Trickle Down:** The supervisor might be dealing with micromanagement, too – from *their* boss. As a result of their own stress about making sure their department meets standards, they may be hesitant to give their staff too much responsibility and control.

- **Questioning Their Own Competence/Usefulness/Abilities:** Though a manager or a coworker may seem confident, they may inwardly struggle with worries about their own abilities, knowledge, shortcomings, how other people view them, or how they compare to others. They may carry the weight of imposter syndrome (*discussed in a later devotion*). Micromanagement presents a way for them to keep proving over and over again that they are indeed competent, worthy of their leadership role, and useful to the organization. In this case, micromanagement might look like one-upmanship. The person who is engaged in this behavior may also view other employees as competition – whether they are or aren't. Competition isn't automatically bad, but it can turn negative when we always view it as *if they win, I lose and I cannot handle losing*. If you happen to have some quality or attribute that the person wishes they had (examples: a particular level of education, great communication skills, or a happy-go-lucky personality), the person may feel "less than" in some way and seek to reinforce their own worth by criticizing the things you do.

- **Perfectionism:** Sometimes, those of us who are perfectionists *(and recovering perfectionists – that's me)* are harder on ourselves than we are on others. However, there are times when we bring enough perfectionism to share with the whole class (or in this case, the workplace). Unfortunately, back when I was constantly trying to meet impossible standards in my life, I didn't understand how my inability to give myself grace for my shortcomings affected my capacity to extend that grace to the people around me.

- **Trying to Control the Only Things They Feel Like They Can Control:** Outside of work, a supervisor may be coping with personal situations and relationships that introduce a level of instability and powerlessness into her life. A manager may be accustomed to being independent and always figuring things out for himself (even when he needs help) or may have grown up in an unstable/unpredictable household in which he had to be the responsible family member.

- **The Team isn't Behaving as a Team:** An employee doesn't seem engaged. He doesn't seem to care about the quality of his own work – or about how his behavior in the workplace affects the team. He may have been trusted with a little responsibility in the past, and it didn't work out well. In other instances, an employee may not be the best fit for her job role or she may be taking longer than expected to learn how to perform her job duties. As a result, a boss may micromanage to try to offset the employee's growing pains. There are times when a supervisor micromanages because he believes he is *helping* the employee.

- **Importance of the Assignment:** Let's say that an employee has been tasked with a work assignment that carries a lot of potential impact, such as writing a grant that could acquire several thousands of dollars for their organization, leading safety training that could prevent severe or fatal accidents, or accurately calculating then distributing funding to people who are in need. When an assignment – and its success – carries a high importance, we can remember that micromanagement (though we don't like it) is motivated by a mutual desire to do the best job possible. There will be times when we just need to get it done and get it done well, bearing external pressures with the help of God.

As employees, how can we deal with micromanagement?

It begins with grace. We remember that our supervisors and coworkers are people like us who are dealing with their own external and internal pressures – and that micromanaging is oftentimes not about us. Secondly, we take a step back and ask ourselves, *Is this person truly micromanaging me OR is he exercising a reasonable amount of authority as my actual manager?* Listen, I've mentioned within this devotional that I needed to work on my relationship with authority figures. I'm accustomed to being self-reliant and doing things my way outside of work – so I had to learn how to *allow myself* to be led by others. Some of us may have come from a workplace with lax or laissez-faire supervisors who let us do our own thing however we wanted, so entering a work environment with managers who are more hands-on (but who are not chronic micromanagers) may give you an organizational culture shock.

Thirdly, we stay open-minded, humble, and willing to listen to coworkers when they describe how they approach a task, especially if they do it differently than we do – they might have a good tip you may decide to try later, *and* they'll feel appreciated.

Fourthly, we utilize opportunities to showcase our great work ethic, our skills, our reliability, and our trustworthiness (opportunities such as when a supervisor is away from the office due to a vacation or a sick day).

We also do as Jesus did when He was challenged. Though He didn't have to do so, He often responded with in-depth information and explanations.

Once, when I had a boss who micromanaged me, I became what I call a *microtasker*. I provided her with status updates on tasks she'd given me. I'd stop by her office to offer additional briefings. I communicated, and communicated, and communicated. I would send professional emails at the end of my shifts, offering bulleted lists of what I'd completed during the workday plus summaries of problems I'd encountered and how I'd fixed them. Originally, she wanted to maintain control over every detail of the work assignments that she gave me, but eventually – through my continuous, proactive updates and perhaps through the realization that she didn't have time to keep up with the minutiae of *both* our jobs, she relented.

With a little shrug, she waved off my latest task update, and said, "Yeah, I know, I know. You don't have to tell me *everything* you're doing. Just go do it. I'll look it over when I have time. It's fine."

Then she returned her attention to her own workload.

In the case of coworkers who *persistently* micromanage – such as those people who try to wield authority like a supervisor without actually being a supervisor, one way to approach this is to tell them that you're going to defer to your actual manager for guidance. Here's an example of how to do this using a trivial topic:

Coworker: It's so important that you have the coffee made by exactly 7:45 AM every morning, and it's best to serve it with rhubarb scones. Never doughnuts. Nobody here likes doughnuts.

You: Thanks for letting me know. I'll be sure to double-check with (insert manager's name) about it.

Obviously, the coworker in the silly example above might be uplifting his own preference and trying to pass this preference off as the "law of the land." *(We will talk more about the people in your workplace who demand that things be done in an exact way – or else they get upset or even angry – within the devotions "Coping with Change Fatigue" and "This One is for the Supervisors: Micromanagement & You & Them").*

Keep in mind, though, that there are people in our workplaces who have unofficial authority – even without possessing a leadership title. As you get to know your company culture more, you'll learn how formal and informal power is handled.

But let me tell you an even better way to approach micromanagers. Be a hype man or hype woman for your coworkers – and for your supervisor, too. What do I mean? Be the person in your workplace who is quick to build up the people around you. Encourage. Congratulate. Cheer for others. While working in a retail environment, I had a coworker who was a chronic micromanager, but I happened to know quite a bit about her life story. I knew her *why*. Her micromanaging stemmed from deep insecurity and trauma. So, while there were times when I needed to be direct and explain to her that while I appreciated her effort, I could handle the tasks that were given to me (i.e. kindly but candidly establishing and communicating reasonable boundaries) – there were other times when I didn't know all the answers to questions asked by customers.

I would turn to this particular coworker while saying to the customer, "I'm not sure, but Sarah here is an expert. She'll be able to help you better with this."

And I meant this wholeheartedly. I used these moments to genuinely build her up.

How have you responded to being micromanaged in the past? Have you ever micromanaged someone else – if so, why? As the key verse discusses, do you believe you can cope with micromanagement with patience and by continuing to do your best?

This One is for the Supervisors: Micromanagement & You & Them

(*or* The Great Micromanagement Extravaganza: The Sequel)

"Be thou diligent to know the state of thy flocks, and look well to thy herds."

Proverbs 27:23 (KJV)

As a supervisor, you may encounter micromanagement via interactions with your own boss toward you, with colleagues and with the people you supervise (especially if you are new in the role), and you may even use it (knowingly or unknowingly) in your workplace.

Can I admit something to you? It is tiring to not only do our own work but also trying to do the work of everyone else around us. You know, there have been plenty of times when I've gotten stuck in the mindset of being too involved with every aspect of Jack/Keisha/Maisie/Danny's work assignments that I start to approach my relationship with God in the same way. I'm not kidding – I have caught myself telling Him that I need so-and-so by this date, and I need that particular provision by the end of the month, and Lord, please review the specifications for the life partner of my dreams so that You and I are both on the same page.

I'm not proud to tell you any of that. Just being honest.

There is a difference between leading and supervising – versus micromanaging. In the previous devotion, I gave a general definition and explanation of what micromanagement is; essentially, it is giving employees very little room and agency (i.e. individual power and influence) to complete the tasks you give them. You don't allow them to take actual ownership of the project, duty, undertaking, or whatever-it-is – even though you assigned it to them and will hold them accountable for the success or failure of the task. It's when we tell them how to do something, show them how to do it, and then immediately proceed to hold their hand while they do it. When we do this, we send the message to our team members that we don't believe they can handle this task without us. We also take away their opportunity to use their unique God-given gifts, background, abilities, creativity, and past experiences in this workplace.

Let's look at how to keep the micro out of management:

- **Make sure your employees receive the training (and resources) they need – when they need it**. Remember how Jesus led the twelve disciples – He taught them through His own actions and behaviors. He modeled exactly what He expected from His followers. Also, consider how Jesus taught the crowds via parables. He knew to break down lessons into manageable and relatable pieces of information.

- **Seek and give feedback.** Whether an employee has been on your staff for a decade or for only a week, welcome and encourage all members of your team to ask questions and suggest ways to make your workplace (or the work they do) even better. Effective communication is an asset in a business (and in life in general).

Build a company culture in which employees feel comfortable with pointing out problems they encounter as they tackle their work responsibilities. If a project doesn't go well or a serious mistake happens, seek answers so you'll know the why *before* automatically assuming that the employee was simply being careless or incompetent. Instead of micromanaging, you can assist the employee with problem solving and brainstorming.

- **Consider whether there is another way to do the task.** Let's say you're training an employee on a process, and the employee says, "Oh, I understand what you showed me, but wouldn't it be more efficient if we did it like *this*?" You pause before answering back, "Well, we've always done it this way. . ." Sure, there will be times at work when you must follow certain steps in a specific way. In that case, you can briefly explain why the process is done this way instead of another way. But there are other opportunities where there is wiggle room to try doing something differently than you've done it before. Stop and ask yourself, *Is it possible to do this task using a new approach – but get the same (or a better) result?* Let the employee know that you hear and appreciate their suggestions. I love telling employees that I like the way their brains work. You can also simply say – while pointing at their head – "I like brain. Brain *good.*" *(Okay, maybe not. Unless you want to).*

- **Give clear instructions, guidelines, and expectations (plus, deadlines).** When we give an employee (or group of employees) an assignment, we want them to take ownership over it. This goes back to using SMART goals, which means goals that are **S**pecific, **M**easurable, **A**chievable, **R**elevant, and **T**ime-bound. Tell them what they are assigned to do – being as specific as possible and tell them how their performance will be rated or measured *(How will they know they've done a good job?)*. Also, make sure to give them the time and resources they need, inform them about why the assignment is important, and give a deadline for when it needs to be finished.

- **Utilize purpose, impact, and appreciation to encourage/motivate the people you lead.** In general, adult learners – and if you work with employees who are grown-ups, then they are *all* adult learners – want to know the *why* behind the tasks they are assigned. I've seen students of all ages who want to do work that has a positive impact on their community. We can help employees to see how doing a great job benefits not only themselves, but other people as well. If we add to this appreciation *(try to be specific when telling an employee why you appreciate what they do)*, team members will be more likely to give their best effort.

- **Reevaluate your ideas regarding who is a leader (and who isn't).** Each person on your team (or in your classroom) is a potential leader in your workplace. There are folks who may not be the most charismatic nor the most outspoken person in the room, but when you give them a work assignment, they get it done – and get it done well. Some leaders are *go!go!go!* all the time while other leaders choose a more relaxed approach. When assigning projects, are you trusting only people on your team who share your same leadership style and personality traits – but micromanaging people who may tackle tasks differently? The Bible offers several examples of people who unexpectedly became leaders and who were trusted by God with major assignments – even though they often didn't speak like a leader, have the background of a leader, nor look like a leader based on other people's assumptions. Seek out the capabilities and potential in all your employees, including those who see things differently.

- **Increasing levels of responsibility.** One reason managers micromanage is because they don't believe or know whether they can trust others with responsibilities. Recall the parable about the ten talents [Matthew 25]. Two of the servants took the money that was entrusted to them and doubled it. They were given the opportunity to show their trustworthiness – and thus, these two servants successfully proved their ability to steward over whatever their boss assigned to them. As their boss told them, "Well done, good and faithful servant: thou hast been faithful over a few things, I will make thee ruler over many things" [Matthew 25:21]. But the third servant did not handle the duty well unlike the others, so the boss decreased his responsibility. It make take some employees longer to become good stewards in the workplace who can be trusted with more and more responsibility; however, some employees may not reach that level and are comfortable with being stewards over the basic requirements of their jobs. How will you know what your team members are capable of unless you step back and let them do the work?

- **Personal and professional development. We can always grow into stronger leaders. Keep growing.** What's your leadership style? Does it fit your current workplace? Were you micromanaged at a previous job? Do you often micromanage your employees – and why? What are your strengths and opportunities for growth as a leader? It's okay to have doubts about your leadership ability. It's also okay to think, *Yes, I struggle with that, but I'm growing and I'll get better at it.* Beyond work, let's also make sure that there is balance in your life. Do you believe you can find or ask for help when you need it? Do you prefer working on a team or by yourself – and if you prefer independence, how can you level up your ability to be *interdependent* as the leader of your team?

Ultimately, supervisors are tasked with one of the hardest but one of the most important responsibilities in the workplace: looking out for the people they lead. The key verse at the beginning of this devotion reminds us to care about the well-being of our team members. If a department in your organization isn't meeting standards, are you willing to slow down and ask them what's going on and how you can help? Let's encourage employees as they become good stewards over what they are assigned – and then let us give them space to do the work.

Stress & Rest

(*or* Overcoming Hurry Sickness)

"And when He had sent the multitudes away, He went up into a mountain apart to pray: and when the evening was come, He was there alone."

Matthew 14:23 (KJV)

Some jobs require employees to maintain a sense of urgency, but what happens when you feel like you must always rush through life? From the moment you wake up in the morning, do you already feel like you're behind? Are you always flitting from one time-consuming commitment to another – never feeling like you have a moment to take a break? Do you feel like you need to *rush, rush, rush* even on your off days?

If you answered *Yes* to any of those questions, maybe you have hurry sickness. Hurry sickness is not a recognized medical condition; instead, it is term to describe the anxious and persistent sense of urgency that some people live with on a day-to-day basis. If you have hurry sickness, braking at red lights or standing in lines might especially aggravate you. You may always feel like you're late for *something*. Being inundated with slow-moving aspects of a usually fast-paced world – like being stuck behind people who are walking slowly at the grocery store, unexpected downtime at work, or anything temporarily interrupting your ability to complete your To-Do list – may cause overwhelming feelings of anger, panic, or defeat.

The classic mascot for hurry sickness would probably be the white rabbit from Lewis Carroll's *Alice's Adventures in Wonderland*. He rushes around – constantly peeking at his watch – while terrified about being late.

In our workplaces, we may be so addicted to that *go, go, go* lifestyle that we often skip our breaks. Or we may eat our lunches at our desks while we tackle more work.

Have you ever felt like you've forgotten how to slow down? Do you hear yourself telling people that you don't have time for rest?

When I was employed in a workplace that I would define as toxic, I pushed myself to work harder and harder to try to earn the respect of my boss and my coworkers. I worked late into the night, I answered emails after hours, and I'd skip breakfast so I could get a head start on work assignments. I stayed so busy that days and weeks would go by without me spending time in God's Word.

Here's the thing about hurry sickness and the unwillingness to slow down: if you don't choose to rest and take breaks, eventually you will have no choice but to rest and take breaks. Every single time that I worked hard for a couple of months – rarely slowing down long enough to care for my body, I'd become ill. Not just for a day. I'm talking about being out for one or two weeks.

Way too quickly, my health – both my physical and mental health – deteriorated. Whenever I needed to call out, I faced self-imposed guilt and shame. I also felt betrayed by my own body. Didn't my body get the memo that I was expected to *work, work, work*? How dare it get tired! How dare it become so exhausted that all I could do was lay in bed all day? How dare it develop new health problems that I didn't have previously! Didn't my body realize how much paperwork I needed to get done?

The importance of rest is emphasized throughout this book. Listen, I know that popular culture tells you that you're supposed to live that #hustle_life: staying on that grind, doing it all on your own, and constantly working *all* the jobs, but Jesus didn't model that kind of life. First off, Jesus delegated and shared the work involved with His ministry on earth [Matthew 9:37; Matthew 10; Mark 6:7]. Secondly, even He took time away to rest, and He knew when to slow down.

We see in the key verse one of the multiple instances of Jesus getting away from everything so He could rest and pray. After He would spend time working – healing and teaching the crowds who came to Him, He would step away to be alone, to rest, and to pray [Luke 5:15-16]. After receiving stressful information, He paused His work so He could withdraw and be renewed [Matthew 14:13]. Even when there was a situation that had a sense of urgency – such as Lazarus' illness and impending death [John 11], Jesus did not get caught up in our world's anxiety-fueled need to *hurry, hurry, hurry.*

Jesus also encouraged others to come away and rest. There was an instance described in Mark 6 in which Him and the disciples stayed so busy that they didn't have time to stop and eat. Jesus had sent the disciples out to serve in pairs, and they were returning to Him after completing the work that He'd sent them to do. What did Jesus do to restore a healthy work/life balance? He commanded the disciples to withdraw from everything and rest [Mark 6:31-32].

Always rushing keeps us from seeing the beauty right in front of our eyes. In the story of the sisters Mary and Martha in the tenth chapter of Luke, Martha stays busy – trying to be a great hostess to Jesus. She is *doing the most*, getting caught up in all the housework and the little details. Of course, the work she was doing was essential – homemaking is necessary and important work. The Word seems to suggest that her sister Mary was helping her *at first*, but then she left Martha with the To-Do list and decided to take a break so she could spend time with Jesus instead. Martha was understandably a bit indignant that her sister was no longer helping her, so she complained to Jesus about it – but He told Martha that Mary's decision to slow down and be with Him was a very good one.

What do you choose to do when you take your breaks at work? *Do you take your breaks?*

Whether you're having a bad day or a year of stressful days, slowing down and resting is good for your body, your mind, and your productivity. May I suggest utilizing your breaks as an opportunity to spend some time outdoors? If possible, take a short stroll outside – around your building – during one of your breaks, have a seat outdoors and take time to enjoy your surroundings as well as the feel of the breeze on your skin, or begin (or end) your workday with a trip to your favorite local park. Even if your shift is usually hectic, try to periodically find even a few minutes to allow your mind time to relax.

If all you can do is push back away from your work laptop for a little while, swivel around in your chair, and then serenely clip a bonsai tree you keep nearby – well, then, get to clipping, my friend.

But hopefully, you take time for the wilderness.

Jesus knew the importance of retreating to the wilderness to rest. You must find your wilderness – that place where you can retreat, be alone, rest, and spend time with God. Maybe it is your home, a room in your home, or your patio. Maybe it's your favorite nature trail. Maybe it's a bathroom stall, a storage closet at work, or an unoccupied room in the building where you work *(No judgment! Sometimes we must get creative about our wilderness spots)*. Regardless of where it is, we benefit from a change in our environment – even a small break away from a difficult workplace or from our pressured routine will do us good. I'd also recommend not spending the duration of your break on your phone, scrolling through social media or news sites.

My wilderness is my fave (mostly empty) public parking lot. I sit in my car with the windows rolled down and peacefully enjoy a hot fudge sundae as I watch the sunset. Isn't ice cream kind of perfect for this devotion? If you don't eat it fast enough, it melts, but if you eat it too fast, you get a headache.

But I don't mind if it melts. God is always nudging me to slow down, so instead of hurrying, I happily choose to rest and savor my ice cream soup.

Speak to Your Mountains

"Jesus answered and said unto them, Verily I say unto you, If ye have faith, and doubt not, ye shall not only do this which is done to the fig tree, but also if ye shall say unto this mountain, Be thou removed, and be thou cast into the sea; it shall be done."

Matthew 21:21 (KJV)

The stress that comes from working in a challenging environment can affect your ability to get a good night's sleep. And if you're also underemployed (living paycheck to paycheck), you may stay up late into the night – worrying about how you're going to pay bills on top of dealing with the tension from your shift.

Y'all, when I worked in toxic workplaces, I felt hopeless, trapped, and helpless. I was grateful for even a terrible job, but I also thought being miserable was what I deserved for not making better educational and career choices. I believed that a dysfunctional place of employment was the best that God could do in my life because I'd messed up so badly by not picking the "right" degree, by not having the right connections, and by not being able to foresee that this job wasn't right for me *(these are all untruths, of course – our Father is a merciful God, and when a door is meant to be opened for us, it will be opened)*.

I would be so overcome by my anxiety, which was exacerbated by draining interactions and exhausting events that happened during the workday – I'd lay down to go to sleep, but I couldn't.

So, I'd put my sneakers on, grab my car keys, and do some solo cruising around my hometown, trying to tire out my anxious brain. Most of those sleepless nights, I'd end up in the empty parking lot outside my office building.

As I sat there, staring at the dark windows, uplifting worship music poured from my radio and surrounded me within my car. Then I would pray for myself and for my family. I also prayed for the one coworker who was kind to me.

And I prayed for my supervisor and for all the coworkers who weren't kind to me, too.

I spoke words of life and encouragement over myself and over the lives of the people I knew, even the people who hadn't treated me well. I welcomed God into my workplace (*I didn't realize it then, but He was always there*). I'd open my Bible and read the Word (*Psalms were my friend*).

Every single sleepless night, I'd get into my car and drive over to that parking lot to pray – to speak to my mountains. As I sat at my desk during office hours, I prayed even more and kept speaking breakthrough, victory, and encouragement over the stressful areas in my life.

Speaking to our mountains – as Jesus described in the key verse – means that we deliberately shift from talking about how big and overwhelming the problem is, and instead, we talk about how great our God is in all situations. We focus on how He sees us and on the truth about who we are in Christ.

Research has shown that nostalgia – in particular, recalling memories from better moments in our lives, especially moments shared with people we care about (Routledge, 2021) – encourages us, comforts us, and makes us feel less lonely.

We recall all the times that God has been good to us, and times when He has enabled us to be good to other people. This is definitely not about longing to return to the way things were – no, the goal here is to be renewed and strengthened by reminding yourself of how faithful He has been, and since He doesn't change, He will continue to be faithful. The prophet and poet Asaph describes how he shifted his thoughts from hopelessness to hopeful in Psalm 77:11-12 when he wrote, "I will remember the works of the Lord: surely I will remember thy wonders of old. I will meditate also of all thy work, and talk of thy doings."

In Psalm 103:4, David – the one who God enabled to defeat Goliath, and who went from being a shepherd to being a king (even though his father didn't believe he had that leadership vibe) – tells himself to remember God "who redeemeth thy life from destruction; who crowneth thee with lovingkindness and tender mercies." Within the psalm, David continues reminding himself about the abundant amounts of grace and mercy God has given him over the years.

David had sleepless nights, too. But in Psalm 63:6-7, he wrote about God, "When I remember thee upon my bed, and meditate on thee in the night watches. Because thou hast been my help, therefore in the shadow of thy wings will I rejoice."

Sometimes, when I need to shift my thoughts from worry to hope, I think of an experience from my past that I'm grateful for – and for every year I've been alive, I verbally recount one thing or experience that I can praise God for. So, if you're 30, you think of 30 moments from your past that brought you joy. You can choose big or small things. As you get older, you get to list even more moments, people, or resources to be thankful for, and give God praise for all of it.

Learning how to speak to the mountains in my life taught me a level of worship that I had never known. When I later joined a highly supportive workplace, I couldn't stop (and still can't stop) praising God for being with me through the rough times as well as leading me to better opportunities.

You don't have to go camp outside your workplace at 1 AM to speak to your mountains. But instead of giving the problems in your life praise by talking about how heavy they are, speak words of encouragement and victory instead. Even if you struggle to believe the uplifting words you say – keep speaking them. Eventually, you will start to believe them.

Do you have a verse that you can carry around with you – one that reminds you of God's power and faithfulness? (If you haven't chosen one yet, you can start with John 16:33).

You Are Not Your Mistakes (*and You Are Not a Mistake*)

"For a just man falleth seven times, and riseth up again."

Proverbs 24:16 (KJV)

Toxic workplaces tend to not handle mistakes well. Flaws, imperfections, shortcomings, and human errors may lead to supervisors and/or coworkers shaming the employee who has committed the mistake. The focus is usually more on punishing and demeaning the worker rather than brainstorming how to fix the problem (and hopefully, take steps to prevent it from reoccurring).

I experienced this. It kept me up many nights.

One of my supervisors would only acknowledge me when I messed up. The rest of the time, she was either talking *about* me unkindly to our coworkers or pretending that I didn't exist in our small office area. I reached a point where I, too, started to only see my mistakes – instead of the good work that I'd done. I meditated on my flaws and on the rancid reactions my boss gave me.

There is nothing wrong with someone letting us know about a crucial mistake that we've made at work. What's important is *how* it's done. Informing an employee of an oversight or mistake should not involve humiliation, abusive language, shaming in front of other people, or any other personal attack against the employee's identity or intelligence.

In your mind, you may replay what went wrong over and over again, or you may be burdened with regrets, wishing you'd done things differently. You might also be incredibly unkind to yourself, feeling like you should have known better and done better.

It's going to be okay. Really, it will be.

We've all experienced regret.

In Matthew 26:31-75, the disciple Peter assured Jesus that he would never abandon him. But when Jesus was arrested, Peter denied three times that he knew Jesus at all. He'd confidently vowed that he would stick by him through anything no matter what, but later, fear led Peter to treat Him like a stranger.

Can you imagine how much shame likely filled Peter?

In Luke 22:62, the Word says that he "wept bitterly."

Jesus knew how much unforgiveness – including not being able to forgive yourself – can weigh a person down. After the Resurrection, He asked Peter three times if he loved Him, and all three times, Peter said that he did [John 21:15-17].

Peter's focus was formerly on himself and on his shortcomings. Jesus gave Peter a new focus: his love for Christ and on serving others.

If you're in a leadership role, it's important to remember that your staff *will* make mistakes. If your department or organization has a history of not handling mistakes well, your employees will likely A) conceal errors, and B) avoid asking for help or additional training. Both responses may lead to bigger problems later.

Not embracing mistakes in a way that leaves shame out of it can also reinforce or create a company culture fueled by placing blame on others, distrust, and poor communication.

Instead, let the employee know that his coworkers (or you, yourself) made similar mistakes in the past. Leave room for the employee to explain what happened so you can determine why the task wasn't completed correctly. Emphasize that you're available to answer any questions that come up about work assignments – and when questions are asked, offer your answers with patience and understanding. If disciplinary action must follow, please avoid doing so in front of other staff members. Finally, encourage employees by pointing out what they get right – even the smaller things.

As Ephesians 4:32 says, "And be ye kind one to another, tenderhearted, forgiving one another, even as God for Christ's sake hath forgiven you."

Ideally, we want employees to feel like they can admit mistakes and hold themselves accountable (as well as be held accountable), then consider the steps they can take to have a different outcome next time and move forward – all while feeling supported by leadership and coworkers.

Time for a short but important side note to my dear perfectionists and folks who feel like they need to constantly say they're sorry – even when they've done nothing wrong: this chapter is not an invitation to apologize for things you can't control nor be accountable for other adults' behavior. It's no good to be overly critical and harsh toward yourself every time you make any little blunder or slip-up at work.

At the heart of this entire devotional is God's love, mercy, and grace – for us and for the people in our lives.

If you're currently ruminating on a mistake you made, I assure you that a mistake (or several mistakes) does not mean that you're incompetent, or unintelligent, or unworthy.

You'll do better next time. Keep going. Keep growing. Keep learning. You've got this because God's got you.

A Fresh Victory Over the Past

"Give unto them beauty for ashes, the oil of joy for mourning, the garment of praise for the spirit of heaviness. . ."

Isaiah 61:3 (KJV)

How we view a challenging workplace can vary from employee to employee – meaning that one person's *What kind of a place IS this?!* can be another person's *I've seen worse! All this chaos looks like an exciting challenge!*

Just like how some of us enjoy mud runs. If you're not familiar with a mud run, it's an outdoor race where you complete a series of physical challenges – all while having to crawl, shimmy, run, or wade through shallow ponds or trails covered with thick piles of mud.

If you don't end up looking like you slept in a swamp by the time the race is over, I'd question whether you had fun at all. The point is to push yourself physically while getting as dirty as possible.

Now, I didn't say that I personally enjoy mud runs. I enjoy the concept of a mud run. I will watch as *you* participate. I will try to not laugh if you lose a sneaker and a sock within a hill of mud that you had to slide down. But I personally prefer a nice, clean, untimed stroll through the park downtown.

I may not be able to cope with certain aspects of my current work environment while my coworker might thrive in it. What I call a bad job might be a challenging-but-doable job for someone else. That doesn't mean that a coworker is stronger or better just because they don't cry in their car during their lunch break.

There are also times when an employee may become numb and complacent within a toxic work environment. Perhaps that employee feels stuck between two discouraging perspectives: *This job – it is what it is, it's never going to get better,* OR *This is the best job I can and will ever find, all I can do is accept things the way they are, even if it's terrible here.*

Each of us has a different threshold for how much and what kinds of toxicity we can handle – and how long we can endure it. Notice that I didn't say *better*, I said *different*. This threshold can decrease or increase throughout our lives depending on the unique aspects about each of us such as our temperament, our learned coping abilities (especially regarding stress), whether we have a support system, and past experiences we've had.

When I started working at one of my worst past workplaces, I was coping with a personal loss in my life: I'd just lost my home of six years due to it becoming a serious hazard to my safety and well-being. As a result of that loss, I had to leave behind many personal items in a hurry including a tea set that my mother, who had passed away before this event, had given me when I was a child.

So, I was a new employee, but I was also a hurting human being who already felt defeated.

I also grew up with a complicated relationship with authority figures. Who were my authority figures? Parents, *all* adults (even the ones who said or did unkind, terrible things), teachers, older siblings, classmates in upper grades, classmates who seemed smarter/prettier/more popular than I, and so forth. I believed everything they told me about myself, even when it was wrong or when it intentionally or unintentionally caused me to experience shame or harm.

This mindset followed me into adulthood. I assumed that anyone who was in a leadership role in the workplace (or anyone who had been at the company longer than I automatically knew better than me about who I am and what I'm capable of accomplishing AND that their feedback would always be guided by a genuine desire to help me become a better person and a better employee.

Okay, you see it, don't you? How dependent I was on seeking out the authority figures and then making sure that they decided whether I'm good enough or not.

People pleasing was a big thing for me. In my mind, most of my opinions and thoughts as well as who I am = wrong, and everyone else was right because they *knew more or had an important title.*

That is part of the heaviness (and untruths) that I brought into the workplace shift after shift.

Can I honestly ask you what old hurts you might be carrying into work with you? What past painful interactions with others might be popping back up in your life every time you drive into the parking lot at your job?

(By the way, I see you out there, sitting in your car – pumping yourself up and bracing yourself before you walk into the building. Take your time, friend. You got this!)

Maybe you're like me: one of the most dysfunctional workplaces I've been part of hurt even more because it reminded me of the dysfunction that I grew up in.

Have a disagreement with a coworker, and instead of talking it out, they give you the silent treatment and a cold-eyed stare for hours? Hey, wait, wasn't that the same way your dad (or mom, or someone else in your family) handled conflict? I know it was for me.

Feels like your supervisor never makes Jane do half as much work as everyone else? Actual favoritism has no place in a balanced workplace, but maybe it had a place at the table in your family.

Neither the dysfunction from your childhood nor the dysfunction you've been onboarded into is your fault. None of this is about blaming anyone, but instead, it is about realizing that there are plenty of times when the dysfunction you were hired into or born into existed way before you arrived.

However, we are each accountable for what we add to the environment we are in. We are accountable for who we are as adults and as followers of Christ. Are you doing your best to not feed into or add to the dysfunction? One way we do this is by becoming more self-aware of our impact within the workplace.

Is it possible that some elements of your current unhappy workplace are uncovering old wounds that you didn't realize you still have? Wounds that influence your perspective and how you interact with other people. Are you still turning to unhelpful or unhealthy coping mechanisms that you used when you were a child?

God is all about restoration. He's big on replacing what was lost, on repairing what is broken, and on redeeming us.

First and foremost, look at what Christ did for us on the cross: our Lord went through an unimageable amount of suffering before death, but then death was silenced by the Resurrection. Each of us receives grace and life instead of condemnation and death because of Christ.

We can look at Job's life: he lost so much, and went through a season of terrible loss, grief, and unfair judgment from his closest friends, *but then* God decided it was time for Job to be restored [Job 42:10].

Let me note that the Word keeps it real. The Word doesn't say that Job or anyone who knew him forgot what he'd gone through. Even when he was restored, he still needed to cope with his grief and his loss. Nobody pretended like he hadn't been through a lot. After he was restored by God, the people around Job finally gave him the comforting that he'd needed [Job 42:11].

And honestly, how could we have a workplace devotional without mentioning *Job*? Sorry, I had to do it.

Moving forward.

Our key verses at the beginning of this section are from the Book of Isaiah. We see how God makes something really good out of something that was broken and destroyed. Not only that, but even the old, forgotten, broken places – as pointed out in Isaiah 61:4 – are restored.

I know there are days or nights when you don't want to clock-in to that job, but for now (**not forever**), you are there. Fortunately, nothing can cancel out God's purpose and plans for your life. Let me be clear: abuse, mistreatment, manipulation, and harm from other people is unacceptable and should not be justified. Any person's words or actions that influence you to turn away from Him are not God-sent [Matthew 18:6].

You are in that difficult, perhaps stifling workplace – but God can fulfill in your life the words that Joseph said to his brothers in Genesis 50:20: "But as for you, ye thought evil against me; but God meant it unto good. . ."

That doesn't mean you can't or shouldn't apply for other jobs, but what it does mean is that while you are in your current job, God can use it to benefit you in the long-term and to help others.

Maybe He wants you to be someone who shines His light in that workplace. Maybe He wants to prepare you for a future position with more responsibilities, including leading others. Maybe there are certain skills you can take with you into other positions in your current company (within different departments) or into your future workplace – and this is the time and opportunity to learn those skills.

And maybe He sees this season as a time to heal old wounds within you.

I know He did that and continues to do that within me.

One of the many things I learned from working in toxic environments was that I really needed to improve the way I communicate and how I cope when faced with tiring, frustrating, painful experiences. While I was growing up, I'd learned ineffective ways to communicate and cope, and it was time for me to grow in these areas.

Is God lovingly showing you any areas in which you can grow, too?

Quiet Quitting & Feeling Unappreciated

"And whatsoever ye do, do it heartily, as to the Lord, and not unto men."

Colossians 3:23 (KJV)

This one is for the hard-working people who feel unappreciated in their workplace.

Since your first week on the job, you've always done everything you can to be the most devoted employee at the company.

Even without being asked, you come in thirty minutes earlier than everyone else to get started on the daily workload. You're always the last person to leave because you're incredibly dedicated to what you do. You often volunteer for extra work, even when you're exhausted mentally, emotionally, physically, and spiritually.

You rarely (or never) use any of your vacation days because you believe that your team and your clients need you to be there every single day. Missing a shift due to illness or taking a mental health day doesn't fit into your plans.

Your supervisor knows that she can ask you to pick up the slack for other employees who are underperforming, and that you won't say *no* (in a professional way, y'all) to adding more tasks to your already overloaded schedule.

But despite how much you have given to the organization, *someone else* gets chosen for the promotion. You just *knew* that position had your name on it. No one had sacrificed as much as you have, but then they chose Cathy.

Well-rested, smiling Cathy.

Cathy, who doesn't stay so busy that she gets to 2PM on a Monday and realizes that she hasn't drunk not a drop of water all day.

Well-rested, smiling, hydrated Cathy got the promotion.

Sure, she's a decent employee, but has *she* been working late into the night on reports? Has *she* been giving 1000% when it comes to serving customers? Has *she* completely tanked her life outside of work for the sake of the company? Did *she* volunteer to plan the company Christmas party – like you did – even though she really, really didn't want to do it?

Feeling unseen and unappreciated, you take the advice to "quietly quit" (Daugherty, 2023).

In general, quiet quitting is pulling back. This concept means that you stop giving that 1000% (or even your 100%) and instead, you mentally and emotionally disconnect from your workplace while remaining an employee there. Sure, you still do your job, but you're no longer aiming to do your best. You shift from devoted top performer to an employee who does just enough.

First, let me start by saying that I completely understand the desire to withdraw when we feel like our hard work and our sacrifices go overlooked.

Secondly, you're amazing. If no one has told you that you're appreciated, I'm saying it now. I appreciate you.

But here's the thing: it's good to be a team player, but it's not good for you to try to do the work of an entire team. It's good to be fired up and excited about doing your job well. It's not good for you to burnout.

Based on other interpretations of Colossians 3:23, I originally thought our key verse meant that I should work as if God is my supervisor and therefore, God expected me to give 1000% all the time at my job.

I believed that it was biblical for me to overwork and do the most until I reached the point that I was exhausted, angry, and bitter.

Wait, though. If each of us was showing up at our workplaces and working as if God is wearing a badge that says Manager-on-Duty, how would that affect how we perform during our shifts?

Would we still push ourselves to become so burnt out that we're even snapping at the office's potted plant? *(Leaf-onardo da Vinci, I'm so, so sorry for that one time.)*

No, we wouldn't. God is the Creator of healthy work/life balance. He saw the need for rest as so important that He himself demonstrated it to us after He did the work of creating the world [Genesis 2:2 KJV], even though He didn't need to rest since He never grows tired. But we do.

If God was seated in the corner office instead of our current supervisor, would we convince ourselves that we needed to stay up all night, worrying about an inbox full of unanswered emails?

No, we wouldn't.

Let's revisit quiet quitting again.

When you were giving 1000% and skipping your breaks, what was your motivation? Was it solely because you wanted recognition from your boss as well as that promotion?

If the answer is *yes* to both of those questions – no judgment from me, friend!

There is nothing wrong with wanting to do your job well, with wanting to be a great employee, nor with wanting to support your coworkers as well as your supervisor through your contributions to the team.

But I believe that you're like me: you also care about the quality of your work. Think of that triumphant feeling you get when you've done your best.

I believe that you also care about the people you serve: customers, clients, students, patients, your coworkers/teammates, and others. Within you is a heart that knows that your work – no matter what occupation you do – has impact.

There will be days when you can't give your 100% – and that's okay. Please don't be hard on yourself. We all have "off-days" – even when we're at work.

Just don't believe that you must be in fatigued, sleep-is-for-the-weak (it isn't), go-getter mode all the time just to prove your worth at work or to outshine coworkers. When I was working in unhealthy environments, I believed deep down that if I pushed myself to my limit, it would lead to my supervisors and coworkers treating me with kindness – instead of with disdain. I also thought that working harder and longer would account for any ways that I actually did fall short in my work performance. This was an old coping mechanism from my childhood.

In a toxic work environment, *not* recognizing and thanking employees for going above and beyond is so often part of the culture.

When we are giving our all, let us not forget our focus.

In Galatians 1:10, Paul asks us to question our own motivation – the *why* that fuels our *try*: do you aim to do your job well solely for people's approval? Are we giving our best only because we want our supervisor to give us a shout-out in the company newsletter? Or do we realize, whether we get that shout-out or not, that God sees us and approves of us?

Whether anyone in your workplace gives you recognition or not, God sees you. He also sees those moments that no one else sees – like those times when you chatted with that older customer, Annie, who recently lost a loved one and who comes to *your* store, looking for a friendly face.

There is someone you interact with at work who appreciates what you do. That person may not have the power to promote you, but God does.

Can you trust that God has good plans for you? (As a reminder, check out Jeremiah 29:11). Maybe you didn't get the promotion you expected, but God knows exactly when and how to place you in a position that is truly meant for you. Also, please know that it's okay to ask for feedback from the people who make hiring/promoting decisions – feedback regarding your strengths and your opportunities for growth. Use that feedback to help prepare you. Be upset, be disappointed, be sad about the loss of something you believed was meant for you (feel what you need to feel).

Then move forward.

After you go get a slice of Cathy's congratulatory cake in the breakroom, think about your *why*. What are your reasons for doing a good job? The answer(s) to that question will help you when you're feeling demotivated.

And if you're falling asleep while eating that cake, please get some rest.

Give your best, but *rest*.

What's Good?

"For I reckon that the sufferings of this present time are not worthy to be compared with the glory which shall be revealed in us."

Romans 8:18 (KJV)

What do you focus on the most when you talk about your current circumstances?

Before we discuss that question, let's return to the two miracles of Jesus feeding the five thousand [Matthew 14] and the four thousand [Matthew 15]. Each instance begins with a need and a focus. Jesus and His followers were surrounded by thousands of people who had come to Jesus for healing. The crowds willingly walked far away from their villages and their homes to seek Him in the wilderness [Matthew 15:33 KJV]. At some point, they ran out of the food they'd brought with them, and Jesus was concerned that they wouldn't be strong enough to journey back to their homes unless they ate first.

We see Jesus and the disciples choose a different focus: the disciples focused on how little they had – how few loaves and fish were available.

They had their eyes on the lack, on the problem; however, Jesus looked up and gave thanks for what they had. He never ignored the need – in fact, He was the one who pointed it out. But He didn't stay focused on the problem.

He instructed the crowds to sit down. In other words, He told them to be still, rest, and wait. Our Lord then took what resources were available and thanked God for what they had: "And He commanded the multitude to sit down on the grass, and took the five loaves, and the two fishes, and looking up to heaven, He blessed, and brake, and gave the loaves to His disciples, and the disciples to the multitude" [Matthew 14:19].

Now, imagine you're in that crowd. You heard that Jesus was in the wilderness – in the empty, deserted, lonely places – so you wandered out there to be with the Savior. When He tells you to sit down, you don't know what's going to happen next. I'm pretty sure that Peter didn't grab a bullhorn and make an announcement to the multitudes about what was for dinner. You probably didn't even know how few resources were available. All you know is that one moment, you were hungry, and the next, you were eating until you were full.

There are three points I'd like to highlight:

- **Gratitude isn't just a buzz word, it is powerful.** Seeing the good in our situations and thanking God for what we *do* have does not mean that we must pretend that nothing's wrong or that we don't have any needs. It does not require that we pretend that all is well if it isn't. But when we give thanks for what is – even if it's less than what we need, we're keeping our eyes on Him. Not on the lack. It also draws God's attention.

In the book of Luke 17:11-19, we see Jesus encounter ten men who suffered from leprosy. Because they were classified as lepers, they were required to maintain a certain physical distance from people who did not have their condition. Therefore, to get

His attention and His help, they called to Him from afar. Without needing to go closer, Jesus heals them as they're walking away. Only one of the healed men turned back around, ran to Jesus, and thanked Him for what He'd done. Jesus called his gratitude – *faith*. Faith closed the distance between Jesus and the man. The other nine men received their healing, but the distance between themselves and their Savior *increased*. They walked away once they got what they wanted, but this one healed man who was overflowing with gratefulness ran *toward* Him.

- **There are times in our past when God delivered us, saved us, or covered us – times we know about, and times we don't know about.** The multitudes didn't know they were about to be fed – they only knew that they were hungry and didn't have food. I think we'd be amazed if we knew all the ways that God has shown up in our lives. He has answered prayers that we haven't prayed yet, and watered areas in our lives that we didn't know were dry. The Word says that He is the God who goes before us [Deuteronomy 31:8]; therefore, we don't need to know all the details of how He's going to deliver us – we only need to remember that He already knows our needs, He knows what's up ahead, and He knows how to take care of us.

- **Gratitude and prayer are a powerful combination**. Here we are – back to gratitude. As Jesus broke the bread, He didn't say, *I really need this to work! Oh, this just has to work! All these people are so hungry, so if this doesn't work out, THEN WHAT?* Instead, He looked up and He gave thanks – then the miracle happened. Have you ever spent ten minutes complaining to God – and called that prayer? Or is that just something I've done? Of course, you can bring all that you are to Christ, and you can fully open up to Him, but we also must include gratitude in our prayers.

There were days when I was too exhausted, too frustrated, and hurting so much that my prayers were only a sentence. On those workdays that were especially difficult, I struggled to see the good in my current situation. Whenever I didn't know what to say to God or what to pray, I'd say the Lord's Prayer [Matthew 6:9-13] – trusting that God knew what I needed, even when I didn't say those needs out loud. Then I would thank Him. There's always something to thank Him for – I'm that person who can spend several minutes thanking Him for letting me enjoy the warmth of the sunlight on my skin or for the wildflowers I saw growing on the side of the road as I drove to work.

We can now return to our initial question: What do you focus on the most when you talk about your current circumstances? Someday, the circumstances in your life will shift. Things will change. Within the key verse, the Apostle Paul expresses a confident hope for the future – he knew that *right now* is not the end of the story.

In Psalm 27:13, choosing the right focus – God's goodness – is emphasized: "I had fainted, unless I had believed to see the goodness of the LORD in the land of the living."

Please, don't keep your mind, your heart, your words, or your thoughts focused on everything that isn't good. Just like Jesus did – *look up.* Bring all your problems and needs to your Father in prayer, give thanks, and then shift your focus to what is good.

When You're Not at Work

Silently Overwhelmed

"Peace I leave with you, my peace I give unto you: not as the world giveth, give I unto you. Let not your heart be troubled, neither let it be afraid."

John 14:27 (KJV)

How are you doing?

When a coworker, acquaintance, or stranger asks us this, many of us answer with a simple *Fine* or *Good* – and we usually ask the person the same question and receive an identical answer. It's an easy answer we can give on autopilot.

Perhaps too often, we ask this question just to be polite, especially if we work in customer service. Sometimes, we ask, "How are you?" – as we keep walking, on our way to somewhere else or to complete the next task, never pausing long enough for our coworker to give us more than a quick *Fine* in reply.

We get caught up in busyness, and whether we want to do so or not, we learned that to be a professional adult, you must A) Sum up how you're feeling into one or two words *(despite how even a status update on the website formerly known as Twitter allowed 280 words and characters)*, and B) Never tell how you're actually feeling nor give additional information about your life when someone asks you, even when people genuinely want to know.

I'm not saying that we should pour out our entire life story every time someone greets us. Feeling comfortable enough to share intimate details about ourselves with the people around us can take time and the building of trust. And that's okay.

Right now, let's live beyond that as we set our eyes on Jesus and on our relationship with Him: How are you doing? I mean, *really*?

Isn't it wonderful that we can honestly pour out how we feel – and talk about what's going on in our lives with our Savior?

You might have been told that God, who created the universe, would be too busy to care about the seemingly "little" things happening in your daily life – but He *does* care.

He is God, who knows exactly how many strands of hair you have growing on your head [Luke 12:7].

He is God, who tells us that He wrote our names on His palm [Isaiah 49:15] – because to Him, we are unforgettable.

He is God, who created every animal and then patiently waited with anticipation as Adam named each one [Genesis 2:19].

He is God, who sent an angel to Elijah – who was *so over* everything, deeply depressed, and overcome with anxiety – and the angel commanded exhausted Elijah to eat (as well as brought food to him) [1 Kings 19: 1-8]. God knows that we can reach a point when we are so overwhelmed and discouraged that we struggle to take care of our basic needs.

Have you ever felt so tired and overwhelmed like that?

You might be smiling and laughing, but on the inside, you may feel anxious, burdened, lonely, tired, discouraged, unmotivated, and emotionally exhausted. There are plenty of us who avoid ever talking about what's going on within us (even with people who truly do want to know the real answer). Sometimes, we don't ask for help because we may fear that we'll be a burden to someone else or because we don't know if anyone will be there for us if we *do* reach out. We may worry that opening up and saying that we need help or asking for someone to be with us through a difficult time might make us look weak, needy, or immature.

Popular culture, especially in a Western society like here in the United States, tells us to value not needing anyone. To do it all ourselves. Be a strong, self-made man or a strong, totally independent woman at all times. Though there is nothing wrong with being strong nor independent – our own strength and our self-reliance has a limit.

Maybe you're anxious or worried about the future.

Jesus Christ often talked about His death and His Resurrection with the disciples – *before* these two events happened. He always knew what was going to come next.

You may avoid opening up and telling anyone that you're struggling – or you may be hesitant to allow people to be with you or to encourage you when you're hurting. Because strong, independent adults are supposed to suffer alone, right?

On the night Jesus was to be arrested, He took His disciples to the garden of Gethsemane. He told most of them to sit down and wait for Him, but then He took three of them – Peter (formerly called Simon, but Jesus renamed him Peter, which means *rock*) as well as James and John (the sons of Zebedee aka the "Sons of Thunder" – a title that Jesus gave to them) – further along with Him.

Then Jesus opened up to these three disciples. He said, "My soul is exceeding sorrowful, even unto death: tarry ye here, and watch with me." [Matthew 26:38]. Then He walked away (not too far), and He prayed. As He prayed, the Word says that He was in so much agony over what was going to happen next – His arrest, His trial, and His crucifixion – that "His sweat was as it were great drops of blood falling down to the ground" [Luke 22:44].

Not only did Jesus experience emotions, but He exhibited a willingness to be vulnerable. Right before His arrest, He prayed three times – laying everything that He felt at God's feet. He also asked Peter, James, and John to stay awake with Him, to sit with Him, to tarry with Him while He carried the incredibly heavy weight of what was about to happen.

Even further, He gave these disciples grace for not being able to stay awake and keep watch with Him.

Do you see what I'm trying to share with you?

Please don't live your life constantly bottling up what you're feeling. If you're struggling or going through a difficult time, open up. Tell someone. Tell as much as you feel comfortable sharing. And if the person you share with doesn't offer the supportive response that you expect or need, give them grace just like Jesus did when He forgave the disciples for falling asleep when He asked them to keep watch with Him. As followers of Christ, we are called to help bear each other's burdens [Galatians 6:2] – as much as we are able to do so. Don't be overcome with guilt if someone is dealing with something that is too heavy for you to carry or too heavy for you to help carry. Ultimately, Christ is the only One who can carry everything we bring to Him – and only He can give us the abundant peace and rest that we need.

Most importantly, pray. Pour out everything you're thinking and feeling to God. He will not get overwhelmed as you lay it all at His feet. There's nothing you can say that will surprise Him nor is there anything you can tell Him that will change His love for you.

The next time you ask someone, "How are you?" – do you think you can pause, look the person in the eyes, and patiently wait for their answer?

Feeling Left Behind & Off-Track

(*or* Who is Your Shepherd?)

"Peter seeing him saith to Jesus, Lord, and what shall this man do?"

John 21:21 (KJV)

Doesn't it seem like whenever we're going through a season of uncertainty, loneliness, feeling lost, or one in which we are waiting on God to take care of a particular need – the lives of the people around us seem to overflow with success?

While you're questioning whether you'll ever meet someone wonderful, your eight sisters just got married, your memaw just got remarried, and your Aunt Sally's Pembroke Welsh Corgi – Biscuit – just got engaged. While you're struggling to pay the rent, your social media feed is packed full of photos featuring old high school friends posing in front of their just-purchased houses. While you and your spouse are praying for a child, you receive invites to baby showers every week. While you're underemployed, unemployed, or working a job that stresses you out every day, you receive news of your peers' college graduations, job offers with amazing salaries and benefits packages, or luxurious vacations around the world.

That was a lot, wasn't it?

Listen, there was a year in which two of my sisters *and* my dad each bought brand-new homes – while I was using a split-payment (two debit cards) to afford a three-dollar cupcake. I'm also the only daughter who *never* brings a significant other to my family's holiday dinners. I'd always wondered why my life had never followed the same path as my friends and siblings.

Surely, I was doing something wrong, right?

Even during seasons in which I sensed and was convicted that I was exactly where God wanted me to be, there were days, weeks, or months in which I focused on O.P.B.s (Other People's Blessings). While feeling bad about myself as I compared my life with the lives of others, I'd think, *Since they have all of that, why don't I?! Is it because I don't work hard enough, make all the right choices, or because I'm unlovable? Why haven't you blessed me like that, Lord? I was supposed to be married with a family and a cute dog way before I reached this age. I'm supposed to have a wildly successful career by now. My life is completely off-track! What should I do? How do I fix it?*

Sure, I was happy for the people around me to be blessed so much *(or at least, I was happy for them 85% of the time – if I'm being honest)*, but I viewed each of their successes as a nagging reminder of how far behind I was in life.

Pause.

I think we've discussed that perspective enough. Let's talk about the truth now.

Many of the beliefs we carry regarding when milestones in our lives are supposed to happen are not based on God's plans for us. Instead, we often judge our own timelines according to the timelines of strangers, acquaintances, our peers, and our family members. Metaphorically, we listen to the directions spouted out by someone else's GPS – which is programmed to tell her how to get where she needs to go, and then we wonder why we feel lost when we follow *those* directions. We refer to the path marked in red ink on someone else's map, and then we feel off-track when we follow it.

God never intended for us to focus on someone else's path nor abandon the path that He has for each of us.

After the Resurrection, a risen Jesus visited Peter and several of the disciples (including John) beside the Sea of Galilee [John 21]. Once He had fed them, He told Peter about what was ahead of him – specifically, how Peter's death would occur. Then He commanded Peter to follow Him. Peter, characteristically outspoken, looked back at the disciple John and asked Jesus, *Okay. . .but what about him, Lord?*

As shown in the key verse, Peter hesitates, takes his eyes off Jesus, and shifts his focus onto his fellow disciple. He wanted Jesus to first tell him what was planned for John. And Jesus answered, "If I will that he tarry till I come, what is that to thee? Follow thou me" [John 21:22].

Ultimately, Jesus needed to tell him *twice* to follow Him. Our Lord knew that Peter was a lot like us: we can get so distracted by other people and by what's going on around us that we take our eyes off Him. Recall when the disciples saw Jesus walking on the water. Peter said, "Lord, if it be thou, bid me come unto thee on the water" [Matthew 14:28]. Jesus told Peter to come to Him, and while Peter was walking on the water toward Jesus, he shifted his focus to the strong and frightening way that the wind was blowing against him.

As Peter began to sink down into the waves and be overcome by the storm he was in, he called to the Lord to save him – and immediately, He did. Then He asked Peter, "O thou of little faith, wherefore didst thou doubt?" [Matthew 14:31].

Whenever we take our focus off Jesus and choose to focus on someone else's blessings (while envying what they have), we're being led by our own doubts and insecurities. While you're seeing O.P.B.s all around you, you'll probably have overly curious people asking you questions that poke your already hurting heart: *When are you going to get married? When are you going to graduate? When are you going to have children? When are you going to get a "real" job?*

But may I ask you a better question: Who's your Shepherd?

Your friends and peers – are they your Shepherd? Social media and pop culture? Your fears and doubts? A timeline determined by someone else? None of these can be our Shepherd, none of these things can lead us. I know what it's like to feel left behind and off-track.

Here are some ways to overcome this feeling:

- **Keep actively engaging in your relationship with God.** Ask Him to guide you, and remind yourself that He's your Shepherd. Whenever someone asks you a question about your timeline *(When are you going to [insert milestone]?)* and you don't know what to say, you can kindly answer, "It will happen when it's supposed to happen. I'm following the Shepherd. My hope is in Him."

- **Don't shame yourself for feeling envious or bitter.** The fruit of shame is more shame. This entire devotional is based on grace for others and for yourself. Feel the feelings, step away from social media (if you use it), then shift your thoughts and focus back to your own God-given path. Remind yourself of all the ways God has been good to you, and how much He loves you.

Celebrate all the blessings in your life. Cheer for your own victories.

- **Get excited about other people's success when they tell you about it.** Congratulate them. Cheer for them. This may sound challenging, but I assure you – the more you focus on how Christ is working in your own life, the more you'll see the truth: God has a path for you that fits you perfectly. He does not want us to live according to scarcity: there is more than enough goodness and success for all of us. Afterall, Jesus said, "I am come that they might have life, and that they might have it more abundantly" [John 10:10].

- **Recall stories about people who seemed (or who actually became) off-track.** Consider Jonah, who went in the opposite direction than God wanted, and Joseph, who was destined to be a great leader but who was thrown into a pit, sold into slavery, and put into prison first. Also, remember the stories of people who experienced God's best – even when it was "too late" according to the world. Examples include Lazarus being brought back to life, Ruth and her mother-in-law Naomi encountering Boaz, and also Abraham and Sarah who received their first-born child much later in life.

- **Challenge those thoughts that tell you that you're too late, too old, or behind.** Too late – according to who? God is not bound by our worldly concept of "too late."

- **Boldly step into the opportunities that God provides for you.** Trust that if something (or someone) isn't meant for you, God will shut that door and redirect you. Let Him be your light, your strength, and your guidance as you boldly move forward.

Let's be so fired up about experiencing God's plans for us that we don't have time to focus on what other people are doing. Seriously, when you become passionate about what's happening in your own life – you will be so focused on what's blooming in your own garden that you won't want to waste your energy envying what's growing in someone else's yard.

It's okay if your life doesn't look like your sibling's life. Let's get better at abandoning unhelpful comparisons with our coworkers, our friends, our family members, celebrities, and acquaintances. You are not a failure, and you are not too off-track – I know this because you have a good Shepherd. As you make a habit of shifting your focus from your insecurities to your trust in Him, the joy will come. It'll become easier to genuinely be happy for O.P.B.s. So go ahead: before your Aunt Sally reminds you again, be sure to RSVP to Biscuit's nuptials.

Your Worth Beyond a Job (Dealing with Unemployment)

"It is of the LORD's mercies that we are not consumed, because His compassions fail not. They are new every morning: great is thy faithfulness. The LORD is my portion, saith my soul; therefore will I hope in Him."

Lamentations 3:22-24 (KJV)

Have you ever been around someone who is in a romantic relationship and all he talks about is his significant other? No matter what the conversation is about, he finds a way to name-drop his person into the discussion.

I've been like that with jobs. There were times when my life was centered around my workplace and coworkers. I happen to be one of those people who, when the Lord gives me something good, I end up trying to make it the center of my life (if I'm not careful about keeping everything in its proper place).

One of the problems with finding our identity and worth solely in our jobs is because life shifts and changes. Sometimes, we get laid off or let go from our positions.

Then what?

Have you ever coped with extended periods of time in which you were unemployed? I know what it's like. The discouragement. The frustration. The hours spent filling out job applications, and then hoping at least one company will call you in for an interview. Looking for a new job can oftentimes feel like a full-time job. I remember criticizing myself harshly for how long my unemployment was lasting while losing sleep as I worried about how to buy food and pay bills. Shame – and feeling as if I'd lost a big part of what made me worthy and useful – ruled my thoughts.

But do you know what I realized while I was unemployed?

My job was my life. I'd made it my reason for existing.

The only reason I felt motivated to get out of bed in the morning was because of my job. On my off days, I tended to just float along – doing nothing in particular by myself. Okay, that might not sound terrible to many of you. Let me put this another way: when I wasn't working (such as on my off days), I felt useless and lacked a sense of purpose.

So, when you feel like that for only 24-hours while you're employed and taking a day off – naturally, a year or more of "off days" (i.e. unemployment) will feel absolutely painful, especially on an emotional and mental level. Without a job and the steady routine it provided, I struggled with finding a reason to get out of bed. Then came even more unhelpful and damaging thoughts: *If I had a significant other, I'd have a purpose* OR *If I had children, I'd have to get up and keep going instead of letting myself be so lost and aimless,* OR *If I hadn't lost that job, I wouldn't be stuck like this* OR *God knows that I need a job to have purpose in my life and to pay my bills – why is He abandoning me during this season of unemployment?*

Okay, enough of that. Let's talk about the truth now.

If you're currently dealing with job loss and you're hoping for a new job – *it's time for you to bloom, baby.* No, I'm not saying to wait until you're out of this season before you bloom. I'm talking about now – while you're in it.

Do you feel like you've lost your purpose and your motivation since you lost your job? If so, let me tell you something that I learned: purpose doesn't come from what we do or from our job titles, it comes from God and it cannot be taken from you. Yes, we will face delays, setbacks, closed doors, and redirection in our lives. But when we lose something (or someone) that we thought we couldn't live without – and we get to a place where we feel stuck mentally, emotionally, and spiritually *(physically, too – as I mentioned, I didn't see any reason why I should get out of bed or do anything),* God is telling us that something in our lives needs to change.

Maybe He's been trying to get your attention for a while now. When I became unemployed, my life went from *go!go!go!* to *slow, slow, slow*. Honestly, I was not a fan.

Or maybe He's going to use this to show you that He truly does work all things together for your good [Romans 8:28]. This includes using those times when we wished we'd done better or made a wiser decision – but didn't. Even those situations in which we were the ones who messed up, our God can and will use that, too. By the way, that verse – Romans 8:28 – reminds us that even when we feel like we've lost our purpose or our motivation to move forward, He still has *His* purpose for each of us.

So how do you bloom in a season of unemployment?

1. **Realize that it is okay to grieve the loss of a job.** There is a term called *disenfranchised grief,* which is when we want to openly grieve the loss of something or someone, but we don't because other people may think that we shouldn't be *this* upset

(or upset at all). For instance, if our friends know how difficult our job was for us, one of our friends might say, *"You're finally free! Hooray! Let's celebrate! Now you can find something you really like."* That friend might not understand why you're sad to lose a job that you didn't like, anyway. But for you, it's still a big loss. When our grief is disenfranchised, we feel like we must mourn by ourselves or hide our sadness.

2. **Bring your pain, your depression, your sadness, your frustration, all of it to Jesus in prayer.** We can reflect on the job loss (especially if it was due to our own actions), what we aim to do differently in our next job – and then we release those thoughts to God. He doesn't require that our prayers be fancy. He's not asking you to say all the right things. Just talk to Him.

3. **Talk to another person about how you feel.** This can be a friend, a family member, or a counselor – just to name a few examples. Putting your thoughts down in a journal also helps. If you're physically unable to leave your home, you can call people, receive online counseling via your computer, and join supportive internet forums or discussion boards. I remember feeling strengthened by asking friends and acquaintances (and strangers via online prayer boards) to pray for me in the season that I was going through.

4. **Create and maintain boundaries regarding conversations about bills and job hunting.** In my household, we didn't allow ourselves to talk about bills after a certain hour each day. When

I was unemployed, I stopped myself from scrolling endlessly through job listings late into the night. So, maybe your attempt to pick three references at 3 AM can actually wait at least until after breakfast in the morning? Your mind and your body need rest for the next day.

5. **If one of the things you miss about work is having somewhere to be, find another place to visit each day (or as often as you like).** Eventually, I started getting up and going to the library and to a wonderful public park. If I got to the park before 8 AM or after 5 PM, parking was free (if not, it was less than a dollar). You can even take a short walk around your neighborhood. Let me be honest: there were times when all I could do was step out onto my balcony. The goal is to remind yourself that there is a whole world out there waiting for you to come and shine your light – whether you have a day job or not.

6. **Building on the last point, free events were my friend. I started to learn (and am still learning) that earning a paycheck and spending money isn't always required to have an enjoyable experience.** Oh, wait – you may think that you're not allowed to have a good time because you're unemployed. But you're praying and trusting God, filling out job applications, refining your resume, and doing your due diligence to change what you can change, right? Please don't believe that God wants you to isolate yourself and live in a state of constant condemnation and defeat. Go out and connect. While you're having fun, you may also meet someone who tells you about

current job openings at her company – ones that you didn't know about.

7. **Figure out a habit or action that encourages a sense of forward motion.** This might sound silly, but on days when I didn't feel motivated to leave the house, I'd put my running shoes on. Running shoes are for people who need to move forward. As a child, my mom would often tell me to take my shoes off and get comfortable when I'd come home from school. Nowadays, I lace my shoes up to tell myself that it's time for me to leave my comfort zone – even if it's for a quick trip to the store or for a walk outside.

8. **Think of the possibilities that are still (or are now) available.** Losing my job created space for me to examine the rest of my God-given identity and abilities. Is there a new skill that you'd like to learn during this season? What other things do you enjoy doing – besides working? If you can't think of anything, recall hobbies and interests you had before your job kept you super busy. What topics are you curious about? Are there free job-training opportunities in your area?

9. **Seek help for financial worries.** Contact credit card companies and see if you can get a lower monthly payment. If you have student loans, communicate with your loan servicer about lower repayment plans or a temporary pause on payments. Look into community or government-based food assistance. I'm forever grateful to my local food banks for feeding me when I couldn't afford food – and now that I'm able to do so, I donate to food

banks and soup kitchens so I can help someone else. Also, in case you need to hear this: you are not your debt. Your life is worth more than whatever it is that you owe. Your debt and bills may feel overwhelming right now, but please hold on. You already know that life shifts and changes, so life can shift any day now in your favor.

10. **Don't compare yourself to other people.** If you need or want to do so, take a break from social media. *And HEY!* Stop saying those mean, discouraging things about yourself to yourself. It's not kind, it's not loving, and it's not helpful. Isaiah 42:3 says, "A bruised reed shall He not break." God sees that you're struggling, and there's a point when even He's like, *Okay, that's enough of that. My child's already dealing with a lot. Enough!* You need sunlight and gentleness to bloom and grow, little flower. Not comparisons and harsh self-criticism.

11. **Now, here's the most important point: we need to be careful of what we allow to become the central focus and the foundation of our lives.** Does this mean that we can't care about our work, our relationships, or other aspects of our lives? Of course we can and should care. But our foundation and our identity must be built on Jesus, who does not change nor shift. As Matthew 7:24-27, He is the Rock that we build upon, if we are wise.

Now, let's say that you truly are confined to a small space or currently cannot leave home to seek new work opportunities. Ask God to reveal to you what is possible – right where you are. Remember that Paul wrote some parts of the New Testament while he was in prison.

Lastly, the key verse is one that I want both of us to remember when we wake up: even if today feels like just another day, it isn't. Always remind yourself that today is a new day. Every time you wake up, God has a fresh start ready for you. Isn't it amazing that our God and His love and faithfulness is unchanging, yet His mercy and compassion for us is renewed every single day?

This season of unemployment will end. Today could be the day. But even if this season doesn't conclude until a week, a month, or however long from now, trust that God is with you in it. Your worth is not dependent on a job. Even when you don't feel like it's true, God *does* have plans and a purpose specifically for you.

Don't Forget to BLOW (Build a Life Outside of Work)

"Therefore I say unto you, Take no thought for your life, what ye shall eat, or what ye shall drink; nor yet for your body, what ye shall put on. Is not the life more than meat, and the body than raiment?"

Matthew 6:25 (KJV)

Can I tell you something? On my breaks at work, especially if I'm having an especially stressful day, I'll go outside, whip out a long, yellow, plastic tube that I paid fifty cents for (it was on clearance in the toy section of the store I went to) – and I proceed to pull a bubble wand from the tube.

Then I blow bubbles.

It's okay if you think that's ridiculous, silly, or childish. Believe me, it has caused passersby to pause and stare at me (a grown woman who looks like she should be very serious) as I happily take a deep breath before exhaling through my pursed lips. My exhale causes a cloud of clear orbs filled with sunlight and patched with rainbow streaks of color to float around me, toward the sky, and to gently seek the attention of playful strangers who want to poke their round, transparent tummies *(apparently, people of all ages get a laugh out of poking bubbles)*.

Kids who pass by love my bubbles. Adults love my bubbles just as much.

As I look up and watch the bubbles fly off toward the blue sky, I am fully present in that moment. I don't check my phone because I just want to be *there* – where I am. I want my whole self – my mind and my heart – there. For a little while, I leave behind whatever it was that had me so stressed out. There is only sunshine, the peacefulness of the breeze quietly blowing and the birds chirping, and a *zing* of happiness within me as I remember that it's okay to play. It's okay to take a break from the seriousness and from adulting and from overthinking. It's okay to gain joy from the simple and basic moments in our day.

Sometimes, I won't be thinking about anything except bubbles. Other times, I briefly tell God about whatever I'm struggling with – and then I let it go just like the bubbles soaring away from me. The deep exhales that are required to blow the best bubbles always calm my anxiety (*as should be expected: deep breathing helps my parasympathetic nervous system signal to my brain that everything is fine, that it's okay to relax*).

Thinking of those bubbles, they remind me that I shouldn't forget to BLOW – which means **B**uild a **L**ife **O**utside of **W**ork.

Listen, if you give me a problem, I can almost guarantee that I'm going to make it the center of my life. Every single source of stress, such as a dysfunctional workplace, becomes a GREAT BIG THING THAT I MUST THINK ABOUT AND TALK ABOUT ALL THE TIME UNTIL IT IS FIXED. If you're not like that – then just excuse me, I'm a little weird. It's so easy for me to make worrying my number one hobby, and to build my identity around what's not going well in my life. Every other area of my life (especially the good bits) shrinks in comparison to the issues that are pressing down on me.

If you *are* like me, then let me remind both of us: there is so much more beyond our present circumstances. There is so much more to your life than where you work and what you do for a living.

Your pain is valid. Your struggle is valid. What you cope with, deal with, and are going through is real and valid. There is something about pain and heartache that makes us feel so lost and isolated – I never feel lonelier than when I'm in pain, sick, or feeling weighed down by discouragement.

This might sound odd, but I cannot write a workplace devotional without discussing your time away from work. I know, I know – you might be too tired and disheartened to do anything but work and sleep. However, it's important for us to build a life beyond our jobs – you can build it brick by brick, or even pebble by pebble, but *you must build*.

You need things on your calendar that you're looking forward to. They don't need to be great big things – one of my things in the past was trying out new food trucks in search of my city's best veggie burger. There must be something positive up ahead that balances out coping with the Sunday night scaries (and Monday night scaries, and Tuesday night scaries, and so on. . .) that you feel during your workweek.

You need interactions with people who don't work with you. I probably phrased that super weird, but let's float with it. If you're solely or predominantly hanging out with coworkers, you might slip into the habit of only talking about work.

You need to not be constantly answering texts and emails about work after you leave the office – especially when you should be resting, spending time with family, spending time with God, and doing things that renew you.

You need moments that remind you that there is a world beyond your job. If you're in a toxic workplace, you may become at least a little jaded about your fellow humans. Despite whom you may encounter during your shift (perhaps difficult personalities), there are still wonderful, kind, funny, loving people out there. Never forget that. Despite the workload that may drain the energy and enthusiasm from you daily, there are opportunities to do things that bring you joy – outside of your place of employment. You must seek those opportunities out.

Yes, we should handle our responsibilities in life and at work – but we also must reevaluate how we spend our time when we're not on the clock.

The key verse at the beginning of this devotion *(and the verses that follow it, which aren't listed here – please refer to the Word)* emphasizes how your life and your body are so much more important than what you're worrying about.

Can I be honest again? I'm writing this devotion during a season in my life that is leaving me emotionally and mentally drained. The discouragement is causing me to feel spiritually dry. That's why I'm glad I can look over and see two of the verses I have hanging nearby: "My soul longeth, yea, even fainteth for the courts of the LORD: my heart and flesh crieth out for the living God" [Psalm 84:2 (KJV)] and "As the deer longs for streams of water, so I long for you, O God" [Psalm 42:1 (NLT)].

Jesus was known as a carpenter [Mark 6:3] as well as our Savior. Who better than Him to help you build a life outside of work *(and build your life at work, too)*? There is no better Builder, no greater Foundation.

Moving Up Or Moving On?

So You Want to be a Boss (But Do You Want to be a Leader?)

"And He said unto them, The kings of the Gentiles exercise lordship over them; and they that exercise authority upon them are called benefactors. But ye shall not be so. . ."

Luke 22:25-26 (KJV)

Are you someone who has formal authority to lead, supervise, discipline, and train other employees? Or are you aiming to someday hold a position like that?

Even better question is, *Why?* Why do you want to be a manager, a supervisor, or a boss? Pause for a moment and honestly think about your *why*.

People often tell me an assortment of reasons and motivations for wanting to be the person who runs the whole enchilada *(enchilada, in this case, being the workplace)*. Oftentimes, it is for a pay increase, to obtain a desired job title, or to gain more authority/power and autonomy or control in the work environment. Motivation is typically centered around the benefits that the person would acquire for himself if he stepped into a supervisory role. I completely understand: a promotion should come with additional responsibilities as well as perks.

Now, let me tell you a secret: not everyone who is a supervisor or manager is a *leader*. Not everyone in these roles knows how to, you know, effectively supervise, or manage. Wait. . .that's *not* a secret? You already knew that?

When asked why we want a position of authority, we can slip into the mindset of only talking about why we deserve the promotion, and how this role will prepare us for our future careers – but what about the people we supervise? What does the team gain from us taking a managerial role? Do we want to move up in the company solely because we want prestige and the power to tell other people what to do, or do we look forward to enjoying the personal advantages while also using our power to encourage, strengthen, and help our employees?

Unfortunately, some people do believe that moving into management means doing less work. Of course, a manager must be able to delegate tasks. However, a *leader* knows that she sets the standards for the people on her team. If she wants a respectful workplace, she models respect when communicating with her employees. If a leader wants employees to be diligent, dedicated, determined, and accountable, he holds himself to the same standards that he expects of his staff. He's also willing to admit his mistakes (and apologize, if necessary), request and listen to feedback, and give recognition to team members for their contributions.

Other than pay increases, additional resources, and more/longer breaks or vacation time, there are four things that adults often tell me that they want in the workplace (or in a higher education learning environment):

1) Respect for their knowledge, work and life experiences, feedback, and abilities. People have told me several times in the past: "I like coming to you for help because you don't make me feel

dumb." *(I don't like the word* dumb, *but I placed it here for authenticity purposes.)*

2) To be talked to like an adult or peer, not in an inferior way (i.e. respectful and open communication, which includes being listened to). As I tend to say, *You got to know (or learn) how to talk to people.*
3) Appreciation
4) Active support from their supervisors

So, what do I mean by *active support from their supervisors*?

Tell me if this has ever happened to you. Imagine a Monday that has too much Monday in it. Your department is currently understaffed. The technology you need to do your work is not working – no matter how many times you unplug, plug in, and then turn back on the thingamajigs *(Computers! That's the word I was thinking of. . .)*. There are lights flashing on the printers, but nothing's coming out of them. All the phones are ringing, the waiting area is overflowing with clients, employees are short-tempered due to frustration, and the Glade air freshener's scent has shifted from *Tranquil Lavender & Aloe* to *Chaos & I Should Have Called Out Today* (hint: this smells like burnt popcorn in a breakroom microwave).

Your manager steps out from his office, sees his staff doing their best to cope with the challenging workday – but then he turns around and retreats to his office again.

But if your manager is (or wants to be) an effective leader, he doesn't hide in his office and leave his staff members to fend for themselves. *Leaders* roll their sleeves up and get their hands dirty. *Leaders* see their employees drowning in the murky waters of a very

Monday Monday – and they dive in to help them get safely back to the shore. When your department is dealing with being understaffed, *leaders* pick up the slack.

Whenever employees believe that their supervisor respects them, cares about their wellbeing, and will be there to help them when needed (as shown through past actions), we'll see a stronger and more effective team. We'll witness employees willing to give their best more often – to the company, to each other, to customers, and to managers.

What about people who want to be the boss mainly for the title and the power?

Let's talk about that.

You may have arguing and unhealthy conflict within your work environment. Afterall, the focus of this devotional is dysfunctional, difficult, or toxic workplaces.

In the Bible, we see how the disciples often argued about which of them was the greatest among themselves. They *knew* they shouldn't be arguing about this. At least once, Jesus asked them what they were squabbling about, but they wouldn't tell Him [Mark 9:33-34]. Of course, He already knew what they were fussing about.

Whenever the disciples debated who was the greatest one among them, Jesus explained to them about power and authority. As shown in the key verse, some people want power just to be in control, to be admired, and to have others do the work for them.

But Jesus calls us to be different.

Our focus isn't on worrying whether we're the G.O.A.T (Greatest Of All Time) or not. Our focus is on leading with humility and a servant's heart like the Shepherd.

A person who is only a manager sits at the table, does the bare minimum, and believes he is great simply because of his title. A person who is both a manager *and* a leader is willing to help with the heavy lifting and serve others.

Jesus could have ended all those *Who's the Greatest?* arguments among the disciples by reminding them of who He is. Jesus was the greatest among them, but He also was the humblest. Whenever He did talk about His identity, it wasn't to brag – it was to state the truth and to teach a principle.

He showed us that we shouldn't allow a job title or power to go to our heads. In John 13, He washed the feet of the twelve disciples, even Judas' feet (even though He knew Judas would soon betray Him). Then Jesus said to all of them, "Ye call me Master and Lord: and ye say well; for so I am. If I then, your Lord and Master, have washed your feet; ye also ought to wash one another's feet. For I have given you an example, that ye should do as I have done to you" [John 13:13-15].

People who are new to roles that hold authority over other employees often learn that being a supervisor, a manager, a business owner, or even a leader isn't easy. Supervisors deserve grace, too: many managerial roles don't come with proper hands-on leadership training. The upside is that each of us – if we are willing to learn, grow from our mistakes, and seek God's guidance – can become great leaders if that is our goal. Remember, also, that not all leaders have formal titles.

The business world often talks about leadership styles – one of which is servant leadership, and Jesus is a perfect example of servant leadership. Think of examples of great leaders you read about in the Word or have seen in your personal life: what leadership attributes do you admire about them?

(Also, no shade on Mondays. I actually like Mondays.)

Imposter Syndrome

(*or* When You Doubt You Can Do It)

"I can do all things through Christ which strengtheneth me."

Philippians 4:13 (KJV)

Raise a hand if you've ever been asked, "*Who* do you think you are?"

Usually, we're asked this question when we've finally spoken up and shared our opinion, when we've dared to make changes in our lives to grow and mature, or whenever we do anything that is counter to the identity that folks have come to expect of us. As mentioned in a previous devotion, many people in Jesus' hometown doubted His authority and abilities because they knew His family. They had likely been around as He grew up. Jesus is the Messiah, but all they saw was the carpenter's son [Luke 4:22-24].

That opening question is meant to cause us to stumble. To hesitate. To stop in our tracks. Whenever someone has asked me that question – typically with narrowed eyes and an angry, incredulous tone, I felt a part of myself shrink. Doubts about my abilities and my identity would then loom large in my mind – and I'd become quieter and less brave.

Each of us – at some point in our lives – has feared that we aren't smart enough, talented enough, creative enough, lovable enough, responsible enough, or (*insert your own word*) enough. Maybe you were told that you would never graduate high school or college because no one in your family has ever earned a degree. Or maybe someone told you that you're not leadership material because you're just too quiet. Or maybe you read somewhere that you'll never get married – and stay joyfully married – because statistics say so.

Now, raise your hand again if you've ever asked yourself, "*Who do you think you are?*"

Imposter syndrome is when we downplay our achievements and constantly doubt our own ability to do something – even though we *can* accomplish it and maybe have already accomplished it. With imposter syndrome, we expect ourselves to be experts on day one – and we use any mistake as proof that we don't know what we're talking about or what we're doing. We're disappointed with ourselves if we aren't naturally great at leadership, even though the truth is that leadership is a skill that can be learned and improved upon through experience.

Have you ever backed down from applying for a position because you didn't fit every single one of the qualifications? Or you couldn't accept (or you deflected) a compliment from your boss about your work performance? Maybe you were offered a promotion and a supervisory role, but you turned it down because you don't believe you're qualified enough (even though you've been with the company for years and always do a great job). You think, *They should have chosen someone else, anyway. Anyone else would be way better at supervising than I would be.*

Imposter syndrome leads us to disqualify ourselves. We tell ourselves *No* before anyone else can tell us *No*. We keep ourselves on the bench while a part of us wonders what it would be like to walk out onto the field and play in the game. Even if we're the captain of the team, we *push* and *push* and *push* our minds and our bodies, trying to prove to ourselves and to others that we're good enough to even be on the team.

To overcome this mindset, we must remember that God is always with us. His Spirit is within us. The Word says in 1 John 4:4, "Ye are of God, little children, and have overcome them: because greater is He that is in you, than he that is in the world." Therefore, when you take a chance and step boldly into new territory or into a new role (whether that role is *manager, entrepreneur, spouse, parent,* or any other role), you're not doing it solely in your own strength. Our key verse reminds us that God is the One who gives us our strength.

Secondly, remember that other people who have been in your position also made mistakes. Try to view mistakes as learning opportunities. Also, stay humble enough to ask for help, guidance, and additional training when you need it. Asking for help from mentors and other knowledgeable people is a sign of wisdom, not weakness. This is part of a growth mindset. Even further, take time to remind yourself of what you do well, your past accomplishments, and your ability to learn new skills.

It also helps to encourage other people in your workplace, especially if they are new to the company or whenever one of your coworkers makes a mistake.

Whenever you move into a new role, especially when there is a promotion involved – it helps to get comfortable with being uncomfortable. There may be employees who already know how to do the tasks you're learning, and for whatever reason, they didn't apply for the position that you were chosen for (or you were chosen for the role instead of them). As much as possible, avoid comparing their abilities and knowledge with your own. Everyone had to start at the learning stage.

Sure, you may not be an expert like them at a particular task yet, but you'll get there, too. Think about the unique strengths, experiences, and personality characteristics that you offer to the company.

For instance, there was an internal role involved with training new-hires that I applied for at my organization. There were duties I'd need to learn – duties that a handful of other employees already did very well. However, God has given me the gift of being able to easily connect with newcomers *(I was perpetually the "new kid" when I was growing up)* – a factor that would help me in the position. Also, I had ideas for how to improve certain processes based on what I'd learned throughout my life – both formally and informally, and I truly cared about the staff and the success of the company. In addition, I'd already sensed that God had called me to teach, mentor, and train adult learners – and here was an opportunity.

The path He has for your life has nothing to do with how you compare to other people.

Lastly, let's talk about this idea of us being *enough* versus *not enough*. We, as followers of Christ, don't need to classify ourselves based on these limited measurements. Our identities are never and should never be attached to the word *enough*.

You are marvelous because you are His creation [Psalm 139:14; Ephesians 2:10].

You are loved [1 John 4:9].

You are covered by grace [2 Corinthians 12:9].

You are redeemed [Isaiah 44:22].

You are precious, chosen, and valuable [1 Peter 2:4].

You are courageous [Joshua 1:9].

You are more than a conqueror [Romans 8:37].

And oh, how you shine [Matthew 5:16].

There are so many better ways to see ourselves beyond enough or not enough.

Be patient with yourself. You don't have to be perfect. When you boldly choose to undertake a new opportunity, be willing to keep learning and growing – and celebrate even the smallest victories. That's how you overcome doubts. That's how you conquer imposter syndrome every time it makes you question your abilities or your identity.

Don't forget who you are and who your Father is, friend.

Sing a New Song

"My voice shalt Thou hear in the morning, O Lord; in the morning will I direct my prayer unto Thee, and will look up."

Psalm 5:3 (KJV)

Within the key verse for this devotion, David talks about starting his morning with prayer. He began his day with calling upon God. Notice how he said he'd look up – why does David look up? He was lifting his eyes to God because he expected and trusted God to answer.

God knows what we need and when it is needed.

Through your experiences in that workplace, have you learned more about the kind of work environment that you need?

As a result of my own experiences, I let go of my long-held ideas of what would be my dream job – ideas that were fueled by a need to prove my worth and my adulting skills to the people around me. I thought I needed the corner office, the respectable job title attached to my name, and important work to talk about at Thanksgiving dinner so my family would be proud of me. I thought I could only be happy if I had the right kind of "real job."

(*Real job* is such a popular but invalidating phrase. I usually avoid saying it.)

However, God showed me that a sedentary position in an office isn't right for me. And that the true me has become too talkative and loud for a quiet work environment. I also want a good work/life balance now that I'm in my late thirties – experiencing life, working on personal projects, and building relationships are big priorities for me nowadays.

Remember we talked about organizational culture in a previous devo. Can I tell you something that you may have already realized? Sometimes, a workplace truly is toxic, but sometimes, a workplace may just be a bad or an unhealthy fit for us *(of course, it can be both toxic AND not right for us)*. If your work environment is full of unhappiness, complaining, infighting, disrespect, dishonesty, poor work/life balance, ineffective leadership, cruelty, the rampant sharing of hurtful misinformation (negative gossip), poor communication, shame, and passive-aggressiveness – and it causes you to think, *This place just ain't right. I don't think I belong here* OR *This place ain't right. Let me see how I can make it better* – well, that's a good thing.

Maybe you're meant to be a positive force for change in that workplace.

But also, God is helping you to learn what's best for you based on the unique qualities and gifts that He gave to you.

Here are some questions to consider:

- Would you thrive more at a large organization or at a smaller business?
- Are you more suited for remote work (working from home), in-office work, or a hybrid (a mix of both)?
- Do you excel in a workplace full of unpredictability, a faster pace, and tasks that lack routine? Or do you perform best in a workplace characterized by a slower pace, quietness, and few distractions?

- If there is currently a job that you have your eyes on – does it offer a good work/life balance?
- What matters most to you about a job/career? (Examples: team environment, not stuck at a desk all day, good benefits, purposeful work, etc.)
- What kind of values do you expect and need in your future workplace?
- Are you willing to accept a job in a field that you've never worked in – just to try it out and explore whether it's a good fit or not?
- How much training (or additional training) are you willing to undertake for a future job?
- Can you trust that God knows what He's doing, even when you feel off-track or behind in comparison to your peers? Can you stay flexible and open-minded as He leads you? *(Sometimes, we feel off-track and lost, but we're actually right where we're meant to be. There are times when I feel lost, but I'm actually just* uncomfortable *– and that's not always a bad thing)(by the way, here's a reminder to not compare your path in life to your peers' life paths)*

Trust me: God knows where He's leading you. I've seen Him lead me to exactly where I needed to be, even though it didn't make sense at the time. It always made sense to Him. He took my experiences at dysfunctional workplaces and caused them to benefit me. God continues to work all things together for my good [Romans 8:28].

He is willing to do that for you, too.

So, what comes next in your story, my friend? Sing a new song.

Who Will You Help (When Things are Better)?

"Blessed be God, even the Father of our Lord Jesus Christ, the Father of mercies, and the God of all comfort; Who comforteth us in all our tribulation, that we may be able to comfort them which are in any trouble, by the comfort wherewith we ourselves are comforted of God."

2 Corinthians 1:3-4 (KJV)

I had fifty cents left until payday *next* Friday.

And no more ink in my printer. What I needed was a hardcopy of my resume so I could go in person to apply for a second job at a restaurant near my home. Thank God for our public library – I knew I could print my resume there for fifteen cents a page. I was so grateful I'd found two quarters in the crevices of my car.

As I settled down at a computer to view and print my resume, a young man walked in with a blanket wrapped around his shoulders like a cape. He wanted to use a computer but needed to get a library card first to do so.

The room was so quiet as the librarian said, "Okay, I can help you with that. What's your street address? Where do you live?"

The teenager replied with a gentle and steady voice, "Nowhere at the moment."

"You don't have a street address?"

"No."

"All right. Do you have a phone number?"

"No, I don't – not right now."

He was asked his age: he was a teenager.

Eventually, the librarian obtained enough information, and the young man gained a library card. He shuffled off to use one of the public computers.

I printed the two pages of my resume and left the last of my change beside the printer for the next person who might need it. It wasn't much, but it was literally all I had left. Afterward, I prayed for him.

Outside the library, I saw two people waiting in a U-Haul – and I wondered if they were the young man's family members.

I know what it's like to not have a home address. To have my belongings tossed into a dumpster, stuffed into a storage unit, or piled into a U-Haul.

Oftentimes, after we've been through difficult situations and heartbreaking events, we encounter someone else going through the same trials we've been through – and we see ourselves (or someone we love) in that person.

It may be hard to believe right now, but life will improve.

I know that the frustration, the heartache, the anxiety, and all the mornings and nights when you wonder when things will finally get better tell you that's not true. A difficult season feels overwhelming when you're experiencing it, sometimes it still hurts after you're through it, but my hope for you is that the bad days and the absolutely terrible days will ultimately produce good fruit in your life.

I want you to be able to live above survival mode and move into a season in which you are thriving. If it hasn't happened yet, I am writing this as I think of you and what is possible: working in a supportive environment where you can confidently share your ideas and who you are (or witnessing your current workplace undergo positive changes that shift it from toxic to supportive), blooming even on the hard days, shining your light and God's love in places that need more of your unique sparkle, and moving up into leadership positions.

This is not prosperity gospel. This is hope. Ultimately, I want the best for you – based on what God knows is best for you.

Most importantly, I want you to know, experience – and share – Christ's love and His peace.

In a previous devotion, we remembered how good God has been to us in the past. Always think about those times when you're discouraged and tired.

In Psalm 30:5, we are reminded that "weeping may endure for a night, but joy cometh in the morning" (KJV).

Your night might have been a season of underemployment or unemployment. Your night could be several weeks of recovery from surgery. Your night could have been a decade of homelessness. Your night could be a period of loneliness and isolation. Your night could be the time spent in a workplace that leaves you emotionally drained and overwhelmed most days.

But your morning *will* come.

When you're no longer struggling in the particular area(s) that you're struggling in, how will you utilize your experiences?

Our key verse talks about God's comfort. What are ways that He comforts us?

- By being there for us [Psalm 23:4] [Joshua 1:9]
- By being present with us when we're going through the hardest times of our lives [Isaiah 43:1-2]
- By stepping in and helping us when we have a need [Psalm 145:18-19]
- By comforting us [Revelation 21:4]
- By being a Light in the darkness in our lives [1 John 1:5]
- By caring about our basic needs [Matthew 15:32]
- By giving us strength [Philippians 4:13]
- By giving us the kind of joy and peace that increases our hope [Romans 15:13]
- By listening to us when we are filled with anxiety [Phillippians 4:6-7]
- By being compassionate toward us [Psalm 86:15]
- By being proof that we will overcome whatever difficult circumstances we face in life [John 16:33]
- By guiding us when we don't know what to do [Proverbs 3:5-6]
- By loving us [John 3:16]

Think about what you've gone through. In what ways can you help someone else who may be struggling in the same way?

Fortunately, you don't have to wait until life is perfect to be joyful, grateful, loved, well-rested, and kind. No matter the season we're in or the job title we have, God gives us opportunities to experience joy, healing, and peace right now – and to help someone else.

Since I know what it's like to be the Curve Setter in my workplace, I reach out and help new-hires who are having trouble with learning on-the-job tasks. Not only that, but I offer patience and encouragement as I do. Because I know what it's like to have a bad day at work, I am thankful that God gives me the opportunity to listen to a coworker as she opens up about her challenges or I'll buy a coworker her favorite treat as a pick-me-up. How do I know her favorite treat? I take the time to get to know the people around me.

These are seemingly small gestures, but when I'm going through a tough time, I appreciate every bit of kindness.

Because I know what it's like to work in a discouraging environment, I try to always spread cheerfulness and love to my colleagues as well as to our clients. Even in a great workplace, you never know what someone is dealing with or coping with (or barely coping with). You don't know what the people around you are carrying – not in their arms, but within themselves.

Someday, I hope the people I work with will stop me in the breakroom and curiously ask me why I use my position to serve others, no matter what the position is, and how I can be so joyful even at 8 AM – because then, I can tell them about Jesus.

TL;DR

So, maybe this book is sitting on your TBR (To Be Read) list. Or maybe life currently feels too busy or too chaotic to start a new book right now. Rest. Spend time with Christ through worship, prayer, and reading the Word. Help someone else. Connect with others via healthy, balanced relationships and friendships. And remember that things can and often do get better.

If you need encouragement right now regarding a difficult, frustrating workplace (or concerning another situation):

"Dear brothers and sisters, when troubles of any kind come your way, consider it an opportunity for great joy. For you know that when your faith is tested, your endurance has a chance to grow. So let it grow. . ."
James 1:2-4 (NLT)

&

"These things I have spoken unto you, that in me ye might have peace. In the world ye shall have tribulation: but be of good cheer; I have overcome the world." John 16:33 (KJV)

(These are reminders that joy and tribulation can coexist. We don't have to wait for perfect or better – we can find joy and peace right where we are because Jesus is right where we are.)

About the Author

Vicky L. Rich was born and raised in Huntsville, Alabama. She usually writes fiction and poetry, and she never planned to write a devotional – but she's so thankful that God led her to do it. A balanced life that includes plenty of laughter, joy, and service to others is her aim in life. Most importantly, she knows that there is no stronger power in this world than love – and God is love. She has a BA degree in Communication Arts with a minor in Management and Leadership from the University of Alabama in Huntsville, and a Master's in Education with a focus in Career and Technical Training as well as Organizational Leadership from Athens State University.

But if you really want to know who she is: She's that woman who sometimes puts her foot in her mouth (metaphorically, she's not that bendy). She's that woman who gets too rowdy at board game nights (thankfully, God knows she's rowdy). She still laughs at jokes that a middle schooler would laugh at, she names many of the things she owns (her car is called Bernadette Cooper), and she – like many people – sometimes struggles with her faith, but then God reminds her that His presence and love. She's not a CEO; she's just a rowdy woman who loves Jesus and is loved by Jesus.

Sources Utilized

Devotion: "Gossip in the Workplace"
- Miller, K.D. (2019, August 16). "What is positive gossip?" https://positivepsychology.com/positive-gossip/

Devotion: "Coping with Change Fatigue"
- Soroski, J. (2018, October 10). "What does Selah mean in the Bible and why is it important?" https://www.crosswalk.com/faith/bible-study/what-does-selah-mean.html

Devotion: "Speak to Your Mountains"
- Routledge, C. (2021, April 26). "The surprising power of nostalgia at work." https://hbr.org/2021/04/the-surprising-power-of-nostalgia-at-work

Devotion: "Quietly Quitting & Feeling Unappreciated"
- Daugherty, G. (2023, February 25). "What is quiet quitting and is it a real trend?" https://www.investopedia.com/what-is-quiet-quitting-6743910

www.ingramcontent.com/pod-product-compliance
Lightning Source LLC
Chambersburg PA
CBHW071359210526
45465CB00001B/173